General Robert E. Lee

Courtesy National Archives

R. E. LEE'S
CHEAT MOUNTAIN
CAMPAIGN

By Jack Zinn

McCLAIN PRINTING COMPANY
PARSONS, WEST VIRGINIA 26287

1974

Standard Book Number 87012-151-0
Library of Congress Card Number 73-84415
Printed in the United States of America
Copyright © 1974 by Jack Zinn
Nutter Fort, West Virginia
All Rights Reserved

*Dedicated to my wife, a true
convert to the Blue and Gray
by due process of marriage.*

Table of Contents

Illustrations

Maps

Foreword

The account of R. E. Lee's Cheat Mountain Campaign is not written with the idea in mind of showing the political significance of the expedition—which would seem to be little—as Lee left northwest Virginia with the Federals in possession of the same territory they held at the end of General George B. McClellan's West Virginia Campaign. No attempt is made to read into the account any speculative "what might have been," if the results had been different, which they weren't.

The major attempt is to show forth the campaign as nearly as possible—within our capabilities—of what took place, along with the human interest and local color attendant to the campaign. We have endeavored to show General Lee as of 1861 rather than the Lee of 1862-65 and to relate the circumstances, events, and factors that almost ended his illustrious career before it had scarcely begun.

Both the Union and Confederate parts of the campaign are taken into account; how the soldiers lived, what they believed, what they wore and ate, the ill effect of the adverse weather, and tonic of the ever present humor of the American soldier of all ages.

Attention is given to the mountains, and to the mountain folks that inhabited the area of operations and were practically forced to live from day to day under two flags.

It is hoped that the long forgotten routes, trails, campsites, picket posts, graves, and fortifications, along with other features of the campaign, may be marked and set aside for posterity, a heritage that truly belongs to all Americans.

The view differs in some aspects with most conventional accounts—especially as to the number of men in the Cheat Fort on September 12, 1861—but with the source material available it is believed this view can be substantiated and should be presented.

Unnumbered days have been spent going over the ground of the campaign and in talking to the many descendants of those who lived in the area in Civil War days.

The letters and reports printed herein are reproduced ba-

xi

sically as written. The paragraph divisions, spelling, grammar, and form being retained as in the original and without the benefit of *sic*.

An exception to the above arrangement are the letters of Lavender Ray—spelling and grammar have been corrected with punctuation being inserted where necessary for clarity.

The Bibliography in Appendix A lists forty-six works cited, while Appendix B lists an additional twenty-seven works consulted but not cited, but which in an overall manner could have influenced the writing.

The portrayals of the mountains on the maps are not meant to be a reproduction of each mountain, but only an attempt to show the mountainous conditions, and the mountain system over which the campaign was waged. These ever present and all surrounding mountains are shown basically only on the map on page 48. For the sake of clarity most of the mountains are left off the other maps with only a representation shown at various spots to indicate their presence. The map on page 142 is from a wartime rendition and shows the Huntersville-Huttonsville Pike crossing the Tygart's Valley River from Mingo to Elkwater three times. Other maps show only two crossings and the exact route of the road in 1861 remains unknown, but both versions are shown.

The maps on pages 127, 144, 155, and 168 show a section of the Staunton-Parkersburg Pike depicted as "Old Pike." Evidently at some time a new section of road was made and some wartime maps refer to it as "General Reynolds new road," but nothing could be learned about this small section.

The Confederate camp on the Greenbrier is usually referred to as such—rather than Camp Bartow as it did not receive that name until after the death of Colonel Francis S. Bartow at the Battle of First Manassas who was formerly captain of the Oglethorpe Light Infantry of Savannah, Georgia.

The Staunton-Parkersburg Pike in the Cheat Mountain and Greenbrier River area is now designated U.S. Route 250 and the Huntersville-Huttonsville Pike is U.S. Route 219 to Marlinton and West Virginia State Route 39 to Huntersville.

Many roads, trails, and paths that existed in 1861 are now obliterated, but much effort was made to reestablish their locations.

It is almost impossible to list all who helped in the work of this book, so to those that I may have inadvertently not listed, it is purely accidental and much to my regret, but be assured that all efforts were much appreciated.

I wish to acknowledge with profound thanks the help of the many people and the availability to me of the facilities of various institutions.

Special thanks to James Reed II, who was my principal researcher, and to the West Virginia University Library.

I appreciate the fine cooperation and help from: Mrs. Sarah C. Gillespie, reference archivist, of the Robert W. Woodruff Library, Emory University; David E. Estes, assistant librarian, Emory University Library; Miss Carroll Hart, director of Georgia Department of Archives and History, and Miss Charlotte Ray of the Civil War Records Section; H. G. Blades, director of restoration and reproduction, Tennessee State Library and Archives; Carlton P. West, librarian, Z. Smith Reynolds Library, Wake Forest University; Mrs. Alice Johnston, membership secretary, Indiana Historical Society; Miss Martha E. Wright, reference librarian, Indiana State Library; Miss Margaret Gleason, reference Librarian, State Historical Society of Wisconsin; Miss Merle Moore, librarian, and Miss Mildred Lawson of the Clarksburg Public Library; the Ohio Historical Society; Illinois State Historical Library; United States Department of the Interior, Geological Survey.

Many thanks to: the National Archives, the Library of Congress, Mrs. Jean Wagner, Tennessee State Library and Archives for help in locating pictures of the various Confederate and Federal officers and to Charles E. McDaniel for his fine work in the custom finishing of the photographs.

For their kind permission to quote from various works we are indebted to: Dr. Donald F. Carmony, *Indiana Magazine of History;* Donald L. Rice, Randolph County Historical Society; Harvey Ford of the *Toledo Blade;* Thomas Butler, Jr., McCowat-Mercer Press, Inc.; J. W. Womack, Womack Printing Company; Mary Jane Fowler, Charles Scribner's Sons; Mrs. Georgene Gordon, Louisiana State University Press; Mrs. Elizabeth Teter Phillips, Philippi, West Virginia; Jeanne C. Smith, University of North Carolina Press.

Performing various services and rendering information, the following people were extremely helpful: Lester Burner, Corse See, Brian Rosencranz, Warrick Gibson, Mr. and Mrs.

Elam Weese, Charles Bell, N. B. Wamsley, Miss Pam Smith, Miss Angela Oliverio, W. D. Sigler, and Mrs. Archie Wood.

Those who own the land where the campaign was fought were most generous in allowing us to do extensive research and included: Mrs. Ercell Cutright, Mrs. Jessie Beard Powell, Walter Smith, Mr. and Mrs. P. P. Galford, C. A. Tacy, Gail Tacy, Reuben Currance, and Jerry Currance.

For the advice and concern of our publishers, Ken McClain and George A. Smith, Jr., and the indispensable proofreading and editing by Mrs. Anna Good, we are most grateful.

Finally, appreciation to my wife who provided the encouragement, usually the patience, and so many times the only willing ear for my "oft told tales" of Marse Robert and the West Virginia Campaign of 1861.

Jack E. Zinn
Nutter Fort, West Virginia 26301

Chapter One
Misgiving in the Mountains

The unsatisfactory condition of military operations on the Staunton-Parkersburg Turnpike and in northwestern Virginia in general during the month of July 1861 was the cause of great anxiety both to the Virginia government and to the Confederacy.

On May 4, 1861, General Robert E. Lee had ordered Colonel George Porterfield to Grafton, (West) Virginia, in an attempt to recruit some Confederate companies from that section and to control the important Baltimore and Ohio Railroad if possible.[1] Porterfield had arrived at Grafton on May 14 and found recruiting rather slow, the people very uncooperative and accomplished comparatively little there.[2]

Meanwhile the neighboring state of Ohio under President Lincoln's call was organizing thirteen regiments of three-month volunteers. This quota entitled the state to a major general and Governor Dennison had appointed George B. McClellan to that post. Porterfield kept a wary eye and a nervous ear on these doings and decided he should burn some bridges on the Baltimore and Ohio just in case McClellan should decide to take the train down to call on him with some Union regiments. This was just the excuse McClellan needed to cross the Ohio River with his troops.

On hearing that McClellan was on the move, Porterfield retired to Philippi on May 28, two days after McClellan had ordered two regiments to cross the river at Wheeling and two others at Parkersburg to proceed from these respective points to a junction at Grafton.[3]

At daylight on June 3, 1861, after an all-night march from Grafton, the Union forces attacked Philippi. The surprise was complete and the Confederates fled town in a complete rout—an action referred to as the "Philippi Races" due to the lack of resistance by the Confederates and their hurried and not overly dignified withdrawal.

Porterfield was shortly relieved of his command and replaced by General Robert Garnett, a promising young pro-

1

tégé of Robert E. Lee, who fortified two positions: one at Laurel Hill (Belington) and the other, the western slope of Rich Mountain on the Staunton-Parkersburg Turnpike. From these positions he could menace the Baltimore and Ohio Railroad, and reported to General Lee, "I regard these two passes as the gates to the northwestern country. . . ."[4]

General McClellan sent a strong Union force under Indiana's General T. A. Morris to occupy Garnett's attention at Laurel Hill, wishing him to believe that an impending Union attack was going to be made at that position.

In the meantime, McClellan moved three brigades toward Rich Mountain and on July 11, 1861, Brigadier General William S. Rosecrans' First Brigade outflanked the Confederates under Lieutenant Colonel John Pegram and routed the force stationed there. Garnett, erroneously believing that he was cut off from the Staunton-Parkersburg Pike, retreated by way of Corrick's Ford (Parsons, West Virginia) and was killed in a gallant rearguard action fought there. The remainder of the two portions of his command, who were not captured, fled by various roads and eventually straggled into Monterey, Virginia.

The ideal military solution to the Confederate problem would have been for them to take the offensive and drive the Federals from the ground they had won and held as a result of McClellan's West Virginia Campaign and to penetrate even farther northward and cut the important Baltimore and Ohio Railroad. The objective in the southern part of western Virginia was to drive the Federal forces from the Great Kanawha Valley if possible.

If the Confederates were to remain in northwestern Virginia and not mount a successful offensive, the defensive requirements had to be considered. It would be necessary for them to control key passes in the mountains and to adequately supply the troops garrisoned at those positions.

The Confederates, under Brigadier General Henry Wise, a political general, had pushed into the Kanawha Valley and occupied Tyler Mountain on the north side of the Kanawha River and the east bank of Scary Creek on the south side of the river, some miles west of Charleston. Their object was to

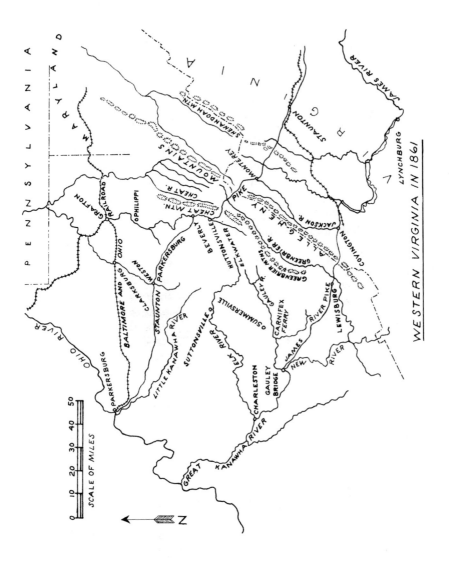

push to the banks of the Ohio River, driving the Federals out of the state, and position the war on its western borders rather than give up a large part of their territory and at the same time endanger other strategic military considerations.

On July 11, 1861, General Jacob Cox with about two and a half regiments of Ohio troops started up the Kanawha River from its mouth at Point Pleasant on the Ohio, and by July 13 had moved to the point where the Pocatalico River puts into the Kanawha, twelve miles below Wise's Tyler Mountain position and three miles below the Scary Creek defense.[5]

Cox attacked the Confederate Scary Creek position on July 17 and was repulsed. On this same date, General Samuel Cooper, Confederate adjutant and inspector general in Richmond, sent General Wise word of the disastrous defeat and retreat of General Garnett's forces at Rich Mountain and Laurel Hill and informed him that General McClellan was reported to be at Huttonsville. He ordered Wise to retreat toward Covington if his position was not essential in Kanawha.[6]

By July 25, Cox occupied Charleston, and on July 29, was in possession of Gauley Bridge, with Wise retreating to Lewisburg and subsequently to White Sulphur Springs. Such was the military situation in the great Kanawha Valley in July 1861.

After Colonel Pegram's defeat and ultimate surrender at Rich Mountain along with Garnett's retreat from Laurel Hill and subsequent defeat and death at Corrick's Ford, the latter's battered command had retreated north by Saint George and West Union (Aurora, West Virginia) striking the Northwestern Turnpike east then turning south to Monterey, while the surviving remnant of Pegram's Rich Mountain force mostly followed the Staunton-Parkersburg Pike to the same town. Richmond authorities frantically moved reinforcements forward, and the command of the Confederate Army of the Northwest was assumed by Brigadier General H. R. Jackson of Georgia on July 14, 1861.[7] He established his headquarters at Monterey, forty-seven miles west of Staunton, and pushed his advance across Allegheny Mountain to the Greenbrier River on the Staunton-Parkersburg road.

Another column, under the command of Brigadier General William Wing Loring, was ordered to the Huntersville and Huttonsville road. Six miles northwest of Huntersville, the road forked at Marlin's Bottoms (Marlinton), the northern fork going to Huttonsville and the southern fork to White Sulphur Springs, where Wise had retreated to; thus holding that point would prevent a flanking movement on Huntersville or other Confederate positions on the north fork of the road.

General Loring, being the ranking officer, now replaced General Jackson as commander of the Confederate Army of the Northwest, July 20, 1861, on receiving the following orders from Robert E. Lee in Richmond:

HEADQUARTERS,
Richmond, Va., July 20, 1861.
Brig. Gen. W. W. Loring,
Provisional Army, Confederate States:
GENERAL: You are assigned to the command of the Northwestern Army, and it is important that you join it without delay. Brig. Gen. H. R. Jackson, now in command of the forces, was at Monterey when last heard from, and he will give you all the information relative to previous operations, the state of the troops, country, &c. You will perceive the necessity of preventing the advance of the enemy, and the importance of restraining him the other side of the Alleghany Ridge. For this purpose you will occupy such passes as in your judgment will effect the object, and your attention is particularly called to the defense of the road leading from Huttonsville (where the enemy is said to be now stationed), through Mailing's Bottom to Huntersville, and the Warm Springs to Millborough, on the Virginia Central Railroad. In addition to the force you will find at Monterey and on the march from Staunton, Brigadier-General Floyd has been directed to move with his brigade upon Covington. Brigadier-General Wise, operating in the valley of the Kanawha, has been directed to move up towards the same point, and Col. Angus W. McDonald, on the South Branch of the Potomac, to Staunton. A union of all forces in the West can thus be effected for a decisive blow, and, when in your judgment proper, it will be made. Such supplies as you cannot procure in your vicinity will be forwarded from Staunton and this place.
Very respectfully,
R. E. Lee,
General, Commanding[8]

Lee followed with another letter the next day giving Loring additional information:

HEADQUARTERS OF THE FORCES,
Richmond, Va., July 21, 1861

General W. W. Loring, Commanding Army of the Northwest:

General: In my letter of yesterday I directed your attention to the importance of occupying the strong passes on the roads leading to Staunton and Millborough, to prevent the enemy reaching the Virginia Central Railroad. The selection of those passes is, of course, left to your judgment; but, should General McClellan not have advanced beyond the Tygart's River Valley, the occupation of the Cheat Mountain, on the Staunton and Parkersburg Turnpike, and the Middle Mountain, on the Huttonsville and Huntersville Turnpike, will hold those roads, from such information as I am able to get, against a large force. The route to Middle Mountain, I am told, is best by Millborough Depot, Pocahontas Court-House, &c., and you are authorized to call upon Pocahontas and Greenbrier Counties for volunteers to hold Middle Mountain, or other passes, and to aid you in driving back the invaders.

I am, &c.,

R. E. Lee,[9]
General, Commanding

McClellan already had Union troops on Cheat Mountain and at Huttonsville when this letter was written but Middle Mountain was still open for Confederate occupation.

General Loring, later nicknamed "Old Blizzards," was an officer of considerable reputation and had been a soldier since boyhood. He was born in Wilmington, North Carolina, December 4, 1818, and in early childhood moved to Florida. At the age of fourteen, he was in the ranks of the volunteers, fighting Indians in the swamps and Everglades. He was not a West Pointer but had a vast amount of combat experience and on June 16, 1837, was appointed a second lieutenant after which he attended school at Alexandria, Virginia, and Georgetown, District of Columbia. He later studied law, being admitted to the bar in 1842, and went back to Florida where he was elected to the state legislature for three years.

In the Seminole war of 1836-38 he was appointed senior captain of a regiment of mounted riflemen, and in the following year he was made major, commanding. He served under General Scott in all the battles of the Mexican War, from Vera Cruz to the city of Mexico, where he lost his left arm, and for gallant conduct, was brevetted lieutenant colonel and then colonel. In 1849, during the gold fever in California, Colonel Loring was ordered to move his regiment across the continent and take charge of the Department of Oregon. On this occasion he marched his troops a distance of 2,500 miles, taking with him a train of 600 mule teams, and held the command of the Department of Oregon until 1851. During five years on the frontier, he fought many engagements with the Indians; then by permission he visited Europe and studied the military systems of the various nations. On his return, he was placed in command of the Department of New Mexico, but during that very year the long sectional quarrel between the North and South changed from a war of words to one of open hostilities and Loring resigned his commission in the United States service to cast his lot with the Confederacy. On May 20, 1861, he was commissioned brigadier general. He was eleven years younger than Robert E. Lee, had outranked him in the old army, and his combat experience greatly exceeded that of Lee.[10]

The Army of the Northwest now included the forces at both Monterey and Huntersville. General Loring reached Monterey on July 22, 1861, and assumed command as of that date, and when he took stock of his forces, he found Colonel Edward Johnson with the Twelfth Georgia Infantry Regiment and Anderson's Lynchburg Lee Battery on Allegheny Mountain with pickets at the Greenbrier River. Colonel Albert Rust's Third Arkansas Infantry Regiment and Colonel John B. Baldwin's Fifty-second Virginia Infantry Regiment were in support distance between Allegheny Mountain and Monterey.

Colonel S. V. Fulkerson's Thirty-seventh Virginia Infantry Regiment, Colonel William B. Taliaferro's Twenty-third Virginia Infantry Regiment, Colonel W. C. Scott's Forty-fourth Virginia Infantry Regiment along with Shumaker's Virginia Battery and Major George Jackson's Fourteenth Virginia Cavalry were at Monterey.

Colonel J. N. Ramsey's First Georgia Infantry Regiment, badly shaken during Garnett's Laurel Hill retreat, and the remnant of Colonel J. M. Heck's Twenty-fifth Virginia Infan-

General W. W. Loring
Courtesy National Archives

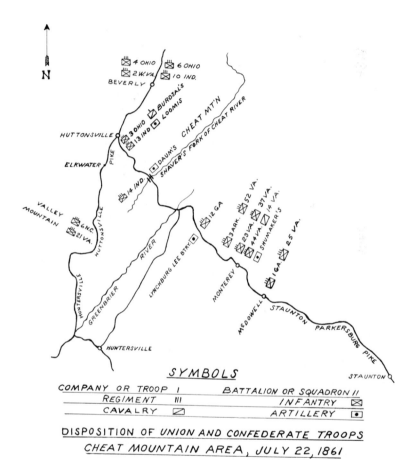

SYMBOLS

COMPANY OR TROOP	I	BATTALION OR SQUADRON	II
REGIMENT	III	INFANTRY	⊠
CAVALRY	⊘	ARTILLERY	▣

DISPOSITION OF UNION AND CONFEDERATE TROOPS
CHEAT MOUNTAIN AREA, JULY 22, 1861

try Regiment, which had been roughly handled at Rich Mountain, were at McDowell for reorganization; the Twenty-fifth at this time being under the command of Major A. G. Reger.[11]

Colonel Stephen Lee's Sixth North Carolina Infantry Regiment (later Sixteenth North Carolina Infantry) and Colonel William Gilham's Twenty-first Virginia Infantry Regiment, with some 2,000 men, were stationed on the road between Huntersville and Valley Mountain with their advance units at the latter place holding the road into the head of Tygart's Valley.[12]

After much urging by General H. R. Jackson, it was decided by Richmond authorities that other troops which had been ordered to Monterey should be redirected to Millborough (Millboro, Virginia) on the Virginia Central Railroad, and thence by way of Warm Springs to Huntersville, (West) Virginia, by a rather difficult but passable road.

A fairly good road ran from Huntersville to the Tygart's Valley, down the valley to Huttonsville and there connected with the Staunton-Parkersburg Turnpike. If the Confederates could drive down this valley road, known as the Huntersville-Huttonsville Pike, before the Federals occupied it in force, it would be much easier than making a difficult and costly frontal attack on the growing fortifications on Cheat Mountain Summit which the Federals had now occupied. Rather, upon gaining the vicinity of Huttonsville they could force the Staunton-Parkersburg Pike and take the Cheat Summit stronghold from the rear and General Jackson was alertly aware of this opportunity.

On the other hand, if the Federals pushed up the Huntersville-Huttonsville Pike and on to Millborough they would be able to cut the Virginia Central Railroad there and stop the supplies that were going to the Confederate Army in the Kanawha Valley from the Jackson River area.

Also, if the Federals were to drive along the Staunton-Parkersburg Pike and occupy Staunton—also on the Virginia Central Railroad—much needed supplies would be cut off to eastern Virginia from the fertile Shenandoah Valley and its vital grain resources. The Confederates had to make every

General J. J. Reynolds
Commanding First Brigade, Army of Occupation of West Virginia.
Courtesy Library of Congress

possible effort to keep this vital railroad operating and in friendly hands.

If the Southern forces took the offensive, the common objective would be the Federal force on Cheat Summit and at Elkwater, a few miles south of Huttonsville on the Hunters-ville road. If the Confederates could bring about the fall of these positions it could open the way for a drive on the coveted Baltimore and Ohio Railroad.

On the twenty-second of July 1861, General George B. McClellan, commanding Union forces in West Virginia, was called to Washington to assume command of the Division of the Potomac, comprising all troops in and around Washing-ton. He had early ordered reconnaissances to be made for entrenchments at the Cheat Mountain Summit as well as on the Huntersville road near Elkwater, and on the afternoon and night of the twenty-second, he gave final instructions for the completion of those works. He turned over the command to Brigadier General William Starke Rosecrans just prior to departing for his new assignment.[13]

Rosecrans, in turn, placed General J. J. Reynolds in per-sonal command of the Federal forces in the Cheat Mountain, Huttonsville, and Elkwater area. A West Point graduate and a former regular army officer, Reynolds knew the task at hand. He had done frontier duty in the west, been an instruc-tor at West Point for several years, and had resigned his com-mission and become a professor at Washington University in Saint Louis. With the outbreak of war, like most ex-officers, he soon found his way back into the military.

The Confederates would need to work their plan quickly, before Reynolds had too much time to throw up defensive works and be reinforced with additional troops, thereby nul-lifying the existing golden opportunity of a rapid Confed-erate drive straight down the Tygart's Valley.

General Loring spent a few days at Monterey inspecting the troops and gathering information; then moving forward, he established his headquarters at Huntersville on July 30, 1861. He was accompanied by his staff, most of whom had been regular army officers and many of whom would become distinguished persons. Colonel Carter Stevenson, the assistant adjutant general, was destined to rise to the rank of major general, in command of Hood's Corps. Major A. L. Long, the chief of artillery, would become artillery commander of the Second Corps of the Army of Northern Virginia. Captain James L. Corley, chief quartermaster, and Captain R. G. Cole, chief commissary, would occupy like positions on the staff of General Robert E. Lee, and Lieutenant H. M. Mathews, aide-de-camp, would later become governor of West Virginia.[14]

Chapter Two
Sanctuary on Cheat

In describing the Cheat Mountain Campaign, the names referring to the Cheat region in use at that time need some explanation. There were two Union positions in the area, that, by incorrect usage of their names, bring about some confusion. Cheat Mountain in this particular area has three tops. The one farthest west was often referred to as the "western top," at the western foot of which was a Union camp called "Cheat Mountain Pass." The second top was called "middle top," "center top," or "Cheat Summit" and here was located the fortified works and blockhouse known as Cheat Fort. Some reports, especially in Confederate correspondence, mistakenly refer to "Cheat Mountain Summit" as "Cheat Mountain Pass," but the pass was located about nine miles west on the Staunton-Parkersburg Pike toward Huttonsville. The eastern top is referred to by Confederates as "first summit," "first top," "eastern ridge," and also Back Allegheny.

The Confederates early realized the Union forces were fortifying Cheat Summit but did not know what stage the construction had reached or its details.

After the battle of Rich Mountain on July 11, McClellan had moved his troops to Beverly, Huttonsville, and Cheat Mountain Pass which was located approximately three miles east of Huttonsville on the Staunton-Parkersburg Pike. He also reconnoitered Cheat Mountain Summit in force on July 14, 1861, with the Third, Fourth, and Ninth Ohio Infantry Regiments, the Fifthteenth Indiana Infantry Regiment, and a company of H. W. Burdsal's Ohio Cavalry. Rumors of fortifications and Rebels on Cheat were running rampant, but neither were found and the troops returned the same day to the Pass.[1]

McClellan had posted the western Virginia detachments at Buckhannon—watching the guerrillas in Upshur County—and the passes on the line of the main Staunton Pike, to prevent

14

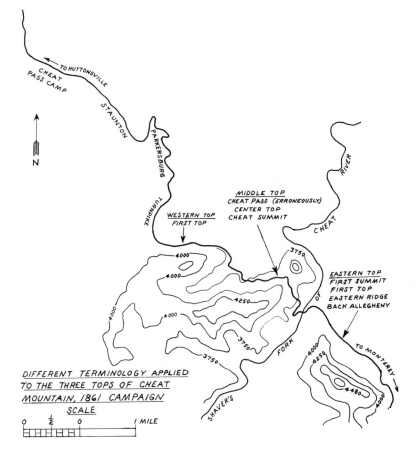

TO HUTTONSVILLE

CHEAT PASS CAMP

STAUNTON

PARKERSBURG TURNPIKE

N

RIVER

CHEAT

MIDDLE TOP
CHEAT PASS (ERRONEOUSLY)
CENTER TOP
CHEAT SUMMIT

WESTERN TOP
FIRST TOP

4000
4000
4000
4000
4250
3750

3750
3750

SHAVER'S

FORK

OF

EASTERN TOP
FIRST SUMMIT
FIRST TOP
EASTERN RIDGE
BACK ALLEGHENY

TO MONTEREY

4000
4250
4480
4000

DIFFERENT TERMINOLOGY APPLIED
TO THE THREE TOPS OF CHEAT
MOUNTAIN, 1861 CAMPAIGN
SCALE

0   ½   0   1 MILE

raids from Tucker, Hardy, and Pendleton counties around the
rear of the advanced positions of the Union forces.[2]

The only practicable road for wheels was by way of Huttonsville and following the turnpike. All supplies except long
forage, had to be wagoned from Grafton or nearby Webster,
about sixty miles—with the road in 1861 almost bottomless
with mud—the problem of supply was extremely difficult.[3]

On July 16, 1861, pursuant to McClellan's preliminary orders and prior to his departure, six companies of the Fourteenth Indiana Infantry Regiment had moved to Cheat Summit to begin fortifying that position. Colonel Nathan Kimball, regimental commander, immediately took steps to cut
off all communication between the scattered inhabitants in
the neighborhood and the Rebel force, as well as to attempt
to gain time by displaying a bold front.

Kimball seized the bridge over Shavers Fork of Cheat
River, half a mile in front of Cheat Summit, and threw out a
line of pickets along the banks of the river, above and below
the bridge. In addition, a strong picket guard was detached in
an area of deadwood three miles to the front of the camp.[4]

The troops soon began to adjust to the new way of life.
New words came into their language. All Confederates were
referred to as "secesh," a corruption of the word secession.
Cheat Mountain was spoken of as "the country God forgot"
and a new daily routine and diet was on hand. A typical
Union soldier's day in western Virginia in 1861 was as follows:

      Reveille—5:30 a.m.
      Wood and Water Call—6:00 a.m.
      Sick Call—6:30 a.m.
      Breakfast—7:00 a.m.
      First Sergeant's Call—8:00 a.m.
      Guard Mounting—8:30 a.m.
      Company Drill—9:30 a.m.
      Re-call—11:00 a.m.
      Wood and Water Call—11:30 a.m.
      Dinner—12:00 m.
      Battalion Drill—2:00 p.m.
      Re-call—4:00 p.m.

Looking up Cheat Mountain Pass from the location of one of the trails from Elkwater.

Dress Parade (Inspection Arms)—5:00 p.m.
Supper—6:00 p.m.
Tattoo—8:30 p.m.
Taps—9:00 p.m.[5]

The baggage of the soldier on the march consisted of: two blankets, canteen, knife and fork, tin cup, haversack and one day's rations, musket, cartridge box with forty rounds, one shirt, one pair of socks, and one pair of drawers. The basic ration was a hard cracker made out of flour and water and called "hardtack," "sheet iron crackers," and various other names.[6] This was supplemented with "salt" or "pickled" fat pork and the indispensable coffee issue. The troops on Cheat Summit breakfasted on "slapjacks" every morning. For many of the other meals, the soldiers could be seen huddled around their fires with the fat pork—sliced and hung on ramrods—sputtering in the blaze, the finished delicacy being formally known as frizzled pork.

These three basic ingredients were prepared in various combinations and cooked different ways. They would dunk the hardtack in their coffee or crumble it up and make sort of a gruel. Some would cook the pork, catch the drippings, and then fry the hardtack in these after soaking it in water. Sometimes ham or bacon was issued, and later on, other rations of a much greater variety, but in the early days in western Virginia, the Union soldier subsisted largely on the preceding and what he bought from the sutlers, one of which accompanied the troops to Cheat Summit.

July 17, 1861, found the Fifteenth Indiana Infantry Regiment, the Third Ohio Infantry Regiment, three companies of the Fourteenth Indiana Infantry Regiment, the Cold Water Michigan Battery of six-pounders, and a company of Ohio Cavalry (Burdsal's) from Cincinnati all encamped at Cheat Mountain Pass with one additional company of the Fourteenth Indiana Regiment at Huttonsville.[7]

Scouting started almost immediately and continued throughout the campaign. Wandering through the mountains became a passion with the men and for days and nights, sometimes for a week, they would lie out in the deep solitude, which intervened between the opposing forces, watching for some sign of life in the enemy's camp, or tracking his scouts to intercept or trap them. Any vague rumor that a few men were wanted to go on a scout would at any time crowd the headquarters with anxious applicants. They had all had their turns on picket duty and became infatuated with the idea of scaling the rugged peaks, which were on every side, and of exploring the deep valleys and ravines, where the silence of the grave seemed to reign.

The regular scouts were regarded with a tenor of reverence, and as they related their adventures around the campfires at night, the young soldiers yearned to emulate their exploits, and looked anxiously forward to the time when they could tell how they had groped their way alone through the laurel thickets. Many of the scouts scaled the summits of moss-covered rocks, slept at night behind a log, watching the clear stars shining above them as they dropped to sleep, to find themselves swept from their resting place by a mountain torrent, which a sudden storm had sent upon them; and after days and nights of privation and suffering, deemed themselves sufficiently rewarded by the sight of an enemy camp on a distant hillside. It might be that some lucky chance would lead them to the discovery of an unguarded path, by which they could lead a party to surprise the camp they had discovered.

Happy then—when a detail was made for a scout—was he who was counted in the number. A few "sheet iron" crackers and a slice or two of ham or bacon were all the provisions needed. The crystal springs, which everywhere gushed from the mountainsides, would supply the water and with smiling faces, they would meet for instructions, and singly, or in small squads, plunge at once into the rocky thickets. Nothing more would be seen of them for days, when, one by one, they would drop in and relate their story to the commandant. Doubtless, some would select a cozy retreat, build a brush tent, and pass the time in fishing; but the great majority were anxious to win distinction, and faithfully performed the duty assigned them. They rarely saw human habitation in their wanderings, and if seen, their instructions

Cheat Mountain Pass looking up the valley.

usually were to avoid them. Their communings were not with man, but with nature, in her most sublime mood.[8]

In Cheat Mountain Pass where Ohio and Indiana troops were camped, the buffoonery and foolishness of the initial state camps ceased and guard duty took on a deadly seriousness. Fifty sentinels paced their lonely beats after taps each night with all fires and lights extinguished except for the guard fire, around which reposed the two reliefs, one hundred men, wrapped in blankets, rifles with fixed bayonets within easy reach. The guard was changed six times nightly, requiring an hour each time for posting.[9]

The Thirteenth Indiana also turned up at the Pass a bit later and Brevet Major Charles Ross said that between fighting Lee, bushwhackers, and rattlesnakes that they had a busy time of it. He declared the snakes numbered in the thousands and related that they were found everywhere, in the streets, in the tents, and in the bedding although luckily no one was bitten by them. Rather to the contrary, one evening while strolling through the camp he smelled a sweet odor, and following the smell to "A" company, found two Frenchmen— members of the company—busily engaged over a frying pan, the contents of which looked like the breast of chicken, but turned out to be rattlesnake. Adjutant Ross, upon invitation to share in the rather rare, though somewhat dubious repast, gracefully declined and quickly found pressing duties elsewhere.

Shortly after, Ross was taken sick and was removed to a house at the head of the Pass. While convalescing, a fifteen-year-old boy of the family would, for his amusement, catch rattlesnakes, and after fastening a string to them—the other end of which was attached to a six-foot pole—would allow them to crawl around the room. The adjutant never could quite see the amusement of the act but his convalescence was hastened considerably.[10]

Camp life took on many varied aspects and found the natives making their rounds in camp with corn bread, pies, and cakes to sell. Lieutenant Colonel John Beatty's servant went out one day and purchased a basket of bread, but returned also with two chickens which he told that officer were gratuitously presented to him, after which, Beatty said he suspected that Fox, his servant, did not always tell the truth.

The soldiers found abundant supplies of huckleberries, blackberries, raspberries, and fox grapes, as big as a man's thumb, which they enjoyably added to their diet.

Humor, as usual, found its welcome way into camp. A private in Colonel Beatty's Third Ohio Regiment wrote home that he had killed two secessionists, and unknown to him, a Zanesville paper published the letter. When the boys of his company read the falsehood they obtained shovels and called on the embarrassed private, graciously and facetiously offering to bury his dead for him, much to the amusement of the entire camp.

One July night the sound of a musket was heard on a picket post three quarters of a mile away, and the shot was repeated by the complete line of sentinels. The whole camp was soon in an uproar and many men, half asleep, rushed from their tents and fired their guns in the company grounds. Others, supposing the enemy near, became excited, tents were struck, Loomis's battery was manned and all awaited the attack, but none was made. It turned out to be a false alarm, some sentinel probably halting and firing on a stump or a tree, thus arousing a thousand men from their warm beds. It was the first night alarm at the Pass, but by no means would it be the last of a long war just started.[11]

Butterfield's system of throwing a chain of connecting sentinels around a command had not yet come into being and would have been impossible to use here, so strong picket posts were established on every road and bridle path as well as keeping out a strong camp guard. Scouting parties of three to six men, under a competent non-commissioned officer, were sent out frequently, and occasionally a lieutenant or captain would make a scout with a larger command. At times these scouting parties would last as long as ten or twelve days and often resulted in serious skirmishes with bushwhackers. Adjutant Ross believed that if a choice had to be made between bushwackers and rattlesnakes that he would have to favor the latter.[12]

Night with its massive silence focused the soldier's mind on the things of home, friends, and loved ones far away. The long rows of white tents forming the encampment, with a chain of wagons behind them—the sight of six brass field-pieces glistening in the light of the moon as it emerged from behind a flying cloud, stacks of muskets with polished barrels aflash as they reflected the guard fire's uncertain light were impressive—but above all, the solemn stillness that reigned supreme in the hours of darkness, moved the mind to home and those left behind.[13]

The camp at the Pass was in a nook at the base of the ascent to the Summit, on the banks of a lovely mountain stream, kept constantly full by living springs above, while in front rose a high rocky and wooded cliff. From the topmost branch of the tallest tree at the top of the cliff, waved the American flag, which Corporal William Nelson of the Fifteenth Indiana had securely fastened there, and in the rear, the gently swelling hills, dotted with open woods grazed by flocks and herds, rolled in park-like splendor fading away until lost in the blue line of mountains beyond.

The pike to Cheat Summit ran along the foot of the cliff in front of the camp, and then began its winding, twisting, way up the bold mountainside. At unpredictable intervals a clearing for a primitive mountain farm let the rays of the cheerful sun fall upon the road—when it decided to shine. Enormous overhanging rocks, covered with moss and vines projected into the edge of the pike and innumerable springs gushed out and the waters crossed the road and fell down the steep declivities on the opposite side. About halfway up the Summit a magnificent scene broke into view, rolling on for miles and seemingly running into a distant mountain range, with a succession of cultivated hills and valleys, interspersed with farmhouses half concealed by the beautiful foliage.[14]

The road was lined with immense chestnut, oak, pine, and ash trees and fringed by a thick undergrowth of laurel, elder, sassafras, and hazel bushes. The soldiers from Ohio recalled that marches up the steep road seriously dampened their military ardor, but like the man who carried the calf until it grew to be an ox, they got accustomed to it.[15]

On July 18, Union soldiers in the vicinity of Huttonsville

Cheat Mountain Pass looking down the valley.

were surprised to see a group of what they estimated to be three or four hundred Confederate soldiers making their way along the Staunton-Parkersburg Pike, totally without arms and seemingly in a state of extremely low morale. They turned out to be prisoners captured at Rich Mountain and paroled by General McClellan who had generously provided them with rations for three days and wagons to carry the sick and wounded. Footsore and weary they were making their way to Monterey.

They camped that night in Cheat Mountain Pass, about a mile from the Union camp and one of the strangest meetings of the war took place as numerous Union officers and enlisted men went over to the Confederate bivouac area and much talk was made about the war, its causes, and why men from both sides thought it was their duty to fight.

Such knightly acts would soon end on both sides and in four years Confederate General Thomas Rosser would march Federal prisoners over this same road in freezing weather and three-foot snowdrifts in their bare feet.

As news of the Confederates' June 21 victory at First Manassas got back into the camps there was great dejection in the Union encampments, while the Southerners reported that their pickets and camp guards made the night air ring with wild shouts for hours when the report first reached their camps.

On July 23, 1861, the military telegraph was completed from Clarksburg to Cheat Mountain Pass, and later from the headquarters there, lines were constructed to Colonel Kimball's camp on the Summit and to Colonel Wagner's on Elkwater.

Paths were laid out through the mountains across which infantry support could be moved from one camp to another in case of attack without marching by the roads. These paths were rough, winding along the slopes of precipitous hills, pitching into deep ravines, leading out at the same steep angle and twisting in all imaginable shapes around the crags, strewed promiscuously on the elevations. Difficult as they were to travel—after the main roads were cut up by the teams—the men preferred them, and soon, except for supply

trains, they formed the chief channel of communication between the camps. The cavalry and infantry were constantly in
motion and at any hour of the day small squads might be
seen making their way over the rough trails, guiding their
mounts along precipices where it would seem difficult for a
goat to climb.

As the road wound its way upward, the character of the
timber changed. Soon the pine thickets shut out the light,
and nothing was seen but the green foliage curtain on either
hand, until crossing a brook at a sharp angle, the opening at
White's house revealed the camp. The tents were pitched on
the slopes of the mountain and their occupants had to prop
their feet against rocks when they lay down at night to prevent them from sliding down the mountain while they slept.
The clouds seemed to rest constantly on Cheat Mountain and
the rain fell daily making for a very dreary camp for the
volunteers from Indiana and Ohio. The slightest breeze
caused the trees to give forth a most melancholy dirge and
when it stormed they howled as if all the demons of the
mountains had congregated to frighten off the intruders who
had dared to set foot on their domain. To add to the dis-
comfort, the soil was a sort of bog turf which never dried out
and though there was not much soil, what there was, soon
worked into a slime and covered the rocks, which possessed
the last clean surfaces available.[16]

By the last of July 1861, the entire Fourteenth Indiana
Infantry Regiment under Colonel Nathan Kimball was encamped at the Summit. Augustus M. Van Dyke, a member of
the Fourteenth, wrote: "Here was the forest primeval, its
murmuring pines and its hemlocks, deep, dark, almost impenetrable, as inhospitable as the caverns that concealed
themselves under the moss that shrouded its bowlders [sic],
where the rain it raineth every day, and it snows in August. . . . To one who loves the wildly picturesque in nature . . . this region could not fail to awe, to please, to fasci-
nate. The great granite bowlders [sic] lie scattered in
inextricable confusion, as if they had fallen from the hands
of giants in battle against each other, and over them there
creeps the straggling, trailing tendrils of what is vulgurly

Old Staunton-Parkersburg Turnpike, eastern approach to Cheat Summit Fort.

called the 'sheep laurel'. Bursting out of the side of the mountain here and there are torrents of living water, that go brawling down the side of the mountain, to fall asleep in the placid, . . . pools of Cheat River, in whose depth and on whose laughing ripples play the mottled mountain trout . . . the sound of axe and the thunder of the falling giant of the forest reverbrated among the hills, and then began the building of an immense fort. . . . The walls were fourteen feet high, eight feet through at the base, narrowing to four feet at the top. These walls were built of pine or hemlock or spruce, cribbiform (if the word is allowable), and the space filled in with earth and stone."[17] Impregnable it seemed to the artillery of the day.

When this fort was finished, another, not so large, was built in the same manner farther up the side of the mountain, and the two were connected by a protected semi-subterranean passage. In the lower and larger one, provision was made for a battery.[18] From this position the artillery could sweep the eastern approach for more than a mile and had an exacting taskmaster in Captain Phillip Daum, the battery commander of Battery A, First (W.) Virginia Artillery.

Both enlisted men and officers plied spade and axe on the fortifications and the tall pines which grew very close together were cut down for several acres, the branches partially lobbed and stripped, and the trees arranged around the camp with the points out. Inside this felled timber a deep ditch was dug. Breastworks were thrown across the road on either side, in a line with the fortifications. In the rear of the fort there was no opening in the forest, except at the distance of a mile or two, an old road long abandoned and almost forgotten.[19] Inside the walls was also a blockhouse and such works were indeed a formidable barrier to any Confederate ambition to take Cheat Summit by frontal attack.

The troops of the Fourteenth Indiana weren't much enthused with their Cheat Mountain assignment or the topography of the country; one of the boys declared that it must have been the place where the Devil's apron string broke when on the way to build a bridge over the Wabash.

The only inhabitant on Cheat Mountain Summit was an

old mountaineer by the name of White who had resided on the lonely spot for twenty-two years. The Fourteenth camped on the White property which J. T. Pool of that regiment described as, "a splendid twenty acre farm averaging ten rocks to every blade of grass." He stated that White was a gaunt, half-starved individual who had never been inside a schoolhouse or heard a sermon until the regimental chaplain had preached a message from his doorstep. Poole thought that he was pious—after his own fashion—his piety consisting in playing "jigs" and "hoe downs" on an old fiddle and shooting hawks on Sunday.

The Fourteenth turned his house into a hospital, his barn into quartermaster's and commissary's quarters and placed the old gentleman himself under arrest. This went very hard with him as he had always been as free as only mountaineers can, but now was not permitted to go out even for the purpose of hunting a stray cow without three or four guards accompanying him. He was a crude sort of blacksmith, but denied having any tools until the Union authorities made search and discovered them. It seems that he also had in his possession several unfinished bowie knives. He was strongly suspected of making the cutlery as well as repairing guns for the Rebels, who had left when the Federals were approaching. Mr. White was forcibly removed from the blacksmithing business and his equipment put to use shoeing Union horses.

When the telegraph was extended up to camp, he became very interested and could understand how a paper with a note written upon it could be strung upon the wire and shoved along, but how to get it past the pole without tearing the paper was a puzzler. When a communication was sent to Huttonsville and an answer returned in fifteen minutes without a paper being strung on the wire, his astonishment was complete and he looked upon the whole thing as witchcraft and upon the operator as one who dealt with the Devil and thoroughly avoided him ever after.

Mr. White was also the keeper of "Hawk Tavern" reputed to be so named by persons other than White, who vowed that hawk was served to diners under the guise of a much more delectable bird. At the tavern was one female employee who

Camp on Cheat Mountain Summit.

baked flat cakes and whom the boys promptly named the "Maid of the Mist." But, those who attempted to woo her found out that she drove a hard bargain, making it a condition that the bestowal of her heart and hand should be in exchange of "Linkin's Skaalp."[20]

Cheat Mountain had an unwelcome visitor make its appearance in the guard tents causing some of the guards to sleep outside in the rain, saying they preferred wet backs to "graybacks." This measure did not long exempt a man, as both "Blue" and "Gray" would soon agree that the little vermin, like death, was no respecter of persons and preyed alike on the just and unjust, moving in all ranks from private to general.

On the mountain at night, the soldiers gathered in groups around the campfires, and "Yankee Doodle," "Hail Columbia," and many other songs would be mixed up with "Dixie Land"—not yet a distinctive Southern song—with a roar that seemed to rock old Cheat to its very foundation. Observers reported that some of the singers had no more music in them than a mule, but made up in energy what they lacked in harmony. Someone in authority decided that type of amusement made too much noise and it was, accordingly, replaced by debating societies and geography classes.

There were also prayer meetings and it was not uncommon to hear songs of praise and thanksgiving to God floating out on the evening air, carrying the hearer back in imagination to old familiar scenes, until one could almost fancy he was sitting in the old meetinghouse, surrounded by family and friends and almost see the familiar face of his old pastor in the pulpit and hear him giving out the opening hymn.[21]

Chapter Three
Bushwhackers in the Laurel

Lieutenant Miliken, with thirty men of Burdsal's troop of Ohio Cavalry, was left with Colonel Kimball's command on the Summit. The infantry scouts had penetrated by mountain paths the enemy's encampment on the top of Buffalo Ridge—the summit of Allegheny Mountain—and the cavalry was ordered to make daily visits to the Greenbrier River running between the Cheat and Allegheny ranges. It was a dangerous service, for there were at least fifty places between the outposts of the Union Army and the far end of the valley where they could be ambushed by infantry and be powerless to make a successful resistance. The Greenbrier glided along the foot of Cheat Mountain, where the Staunton-Parkersburg Pike crossed it, with the descent of the road to the river being steep and literally cut into the face of the out-cropped rock. Below the bridge was a ford, used by horsemen when the stream was not high, and a high rock covered with thick and tangled bushes overhung the ford and had given the crossing the name of "Hanging Rock."[1]

It seems that a group of guerrillas had organized early in the vicinity with a view of cutting off Federal scouts and disrupting Union activities on the road and countryside in general. The citizens preferred their own tried rifles with which they had brought down many a deer and bear in these very forests and thus were not dependent upon Confederate authorities for arms.

On one particular day, eight or nine men with Mr. Ewing Devier met at the home of a Mr. Gum on Back Allegheny Mountain and decided to make an attack against the Federal scouts plying the road. After several hours spent in clambering over rocks and crawling through dense thickets of brush, briers, and laurel, they succeeded in reaching the vicinity of "Hanging Rock" and the bridge across the Greenbrier River at what is now Durbin, West Virginia, and waited there for the enemy's daily cavalry patrol.

The plan was modified after hearing from a citizen of the

Beautiful Greenbrier River.

vicinity, who was near the road the day before and reported, that about forty of the Federal cavalry had scouted nearly a mile to the east of the crossing and returned. Thereupon, because of the possibilities of such a large patrol, it was thought advisable to hold their fire when the time arrived and permit the Union scouts to pass; find out how many there were and open fire if the odds were right. With this in mind, they chose their positions and in a short time eight finely mounted and well-equipped men appeared, moving cautiously down the mountain, supposedly the advance guard of a squadron of cavalry. Contrary to expectation, the horsemen did not come upon the bridge but suddenly wheeled to one side and rode into the stream near the "Hanging Rock" to let their horses drink and cross below the bridge. By this unexpected movement the men in ambush realized their position would be discovered and overrun as soon as the scouts crossed the stream. It seemed to them that their one and only chance for escape lay in firing accurately and immediately upon the supposedly advance squad and hiding themselves before the others could come up.

The horses were quietly drinking, their riders were conversing in subdued tones while the guerrillas selected each his man. One of the troopers drew the reins and started across, this was the signal for opening fire. The report of the first rifle was heard and the others followed in rapid succession and all with deadly effect. Six fell into the water, and when the smoke of the black powder cleared away, they were seen struggling in dying agonies. The seventh was dismounted but was holding himself up by his horse's mane. Two of the party were young and handsome men and were very near each other when fired upon. One was shot first and as he fell forward upon his horse's neck and was trying to hold on, his comrade turned, caught him by the arm and was in the act of leading him away, when a fatal bullet pierced him between the shoulders. Both fell together, their blood flowing in a mingled stream as they struggled together in dying throes and expired almost literally in each other's arms.

The remaining scout dashed across the river, passed the guerrillas without being noticed, but when discovered was

about a hundred yards off, looking as if he was endeavoring
to find out what was going on anyhow. The guerrillas supposing him to be one of a party that had probably passed before
they reached the bridge, immediately took to the woods,
leaving all behind.

As soon as they had thus disappeared, the surviving
trooper dashed back, rushed the bridge, and fled up the
mountain at topmost speed toward Cheat Summit Fort. The
guerrillas returned by the same route which they had come
and disbanded by mutual agreement, returning to their
homes as rapidly as possible.

In a few days it was learned by the mountain grapevine
that Mr. Devier's name had become known to the Federals
and he was advised by friends to evade arrest by keeping with
or very near the Confederate Army, which he did, going with
his son, a Confederate volunteer, to his camp on Shenandoah
Mountain.[2]

Shortly after the ambush, Burdsal's Cavalry was replaced
by a company of Bracken's Indiana Cavalry who took up the
scouting duties in that area.

The Federals continued to step up scouting, and on or
about the seventeenth of July, a scouting party of fifty men
in the charge of Lieutenant Willard of Company E, Fourteenth Indiana Infantry, came upon about an equal number
of Confederates and charged them, killing one or two and
capturing about six prisoners, some camp equipage, and a
large lot of delicious maple sugar which was immensely enjoyed by every member of the detachment.[3]

As Colonel Kimball continued to probe his front, a small
party was sent out led by Lieutenant Williams of F Company,
Fourteenth Indiana, with the object being to break up a
group of Confederates who were in the habit of congregating
at a house seven or eight miles from the Union camp. Williams was able to only partially surprise the enemy and in the
ensuing skirmish one Rebel was mortally wounded and four
prisoners were taken, but they failed to break up the Confederate gatherings. So, in a few days, Captain Williamson with
Company F was sent out with orders to force the position
and break up use of the place. Just as the attacking party was

within musket range, it was detected by the watching Rebels and was able to get in one volley before the Confederates headed for the nearest thickets, which were plentiful. Pursuit was organized and eventually six of the Rebels were captured and the entire party adjourned to the house to inspect the larder, which was suspected to be a supply point of food for Rebel bands. The boys in blue were overwhelmed at the gastronomic delights discovered in the house: honey, milk, butter, maple sugar, young potatoes, bread, chickens, good sweet bacon, and nice fat pigs running about the yard. Stomachs were filled and excess supplies were taken back to Cheat Summit Fort and many a mess had maple syrup, twice a day for several weeks after.[4]

Bushwhacking became quite an issue during the campaign, and as in any discussion as to what is fair in "love and war," became quite controversial.

One Captain Leib of the Union Army Quartermaster Department gave his idea of a typical bushwhacker in West Virginia stating that: "The bushwhackers are composed of a class of men who are noted for their ignorance, idolence, duplicity and dishonesty; whose vices and passions peculiarly fit them for the warfare in which they are engaged, and upon which the civilized world looks with horror. Imagine a stolid, vicious looking countenance, an ungainly figure and an awkward, if not ungraceful, spinal curve in the dorsal region, acquired by laziness and indifference to maintaining an erect posture; a garb of the coarsest texture of home spun kubeb, or 'linsey woolsey' tattered and torn, and so covered with dirt as not to enable one to guess its original color; a dilapidated, rimless hat, or cap of some wild animal's skin covering his head, the hair on which has not been combed for months; his feet covered with moccasins, and a rifle by his side, a powder horn and shot pouch slung around his neck and you have the beau ideal of the West Virginia bushwhackers.

"Thus equipped he sallies forth with the stealth of a panther, and lies in wait for the straggling soldier, courier, or loyal citizen, to whom the only warning of his presence is the sharp click of his deadly rifle. He kills for the sake of killing and plunders for the sake of gain.

Mountain view from Eastern Top of Cheat Mountain.

"Parties of these ferocious beasts under cover of darkness frequently steal into a neighborhood, burn the residences of loyal citizens, rob stores, tanyards and farmhouses of everything they can put to use, especially arms, ammunition, leather, clothing, bedding and salt."[5]

While Captain Leib speaks only of the preying on the Union soldiers and loyal civilians, actually the hated bushwhackers didn't play favorites, and many times exacted their tolls from both sides of the civilian population and the military as well; and were always held in extreme ill repute by the regulars of both armies.

General H. R. Jackson got off on the wrong foot on the bushwhacker proposition when he instituted and condoned the use of such "irregulars" as revealed in his correspondence to the assistant adjutant-general, Confederate States Army, in Richmond written on July 19, 1861.[6] This letter would have ended up on the desk of Robert E. Lee, but the fact that Lee left Richmond on July 28, 1861, makes it doubtful if he ever saw it. If he had, there would probably have been some repercussions as Lee always had a strong distaste for guerrilla warfare.[7]

BRIGADE HEADQUARTERS
Camp at Monterey, July 19, 1861.

Colonel George Deas,
    Assistant Adjutant-General, C. S. Army, Richmond, Va.:
. . . I have also formed a composite command of the Churchville Cavalry, the remnants of the Rockbridge Cavalry, and a company of riflemen, made up from the militia, to which I have assigned Major Jones of the Forty-fourth Virginia Regiment of the Volunteers, an officer who has inspired me with great confidence. They will constitute an advance guard and will be thrown along the turnpike road as near to the enemy as may be safe, to watch his movements, to intercept marauding parties, and the riflemen, who are familiar with the country, to annoy the enemy from the hills and bushes. This rifle corps, some eighty strong, are the picked men of the one hundred and eighty militia who reported for duty: but who on account of the state of their crops, were exceedingly reluctant to leave home. I offered, upon condition for, to allow the others to go home for the purpose of reaping the crops of all. This proposition was cheerfully acceeded to, and I am really in hopes that an efficient corps has been put in the field. . . .[8]

By the time information had filtered back to the Union soldier, Colonel Edward Johnson, who commanded the Confederate camp on Buffalo Ridge of Allegheny Mountain, got most of the credit or discredit for the use of the militia as guerrillas. One Indiana soldier wrote: "They were to report to him, and receive from him their orders. They were to repair to the designated rendezvous, armed with squirrel rifles, and were to be distinguished, while in active service, by strips of white cotton cloth, sewed across their hats or caps. The mountains were soon infested with them. Their orders were to lie in wait behind the rocks, and in the bushes, and shoot Union soldiers as they passed. When captured, they invariably told the same story, that Colonel Johnson's orders were to spare no one wearing a Federal uniform; and whenever any such were seen, to shoot and run. To the credit of the regular Confederate soldiers, it must be said, they denounced these proceedings, and often refused to support the 'bushwhackers' in their murderous plots. When General Lee arrived and assumed command, he opposed the guerrilla system of warfare, and held it in check in his immediate front; but around the foot of Cheat Mountain the 'bushwhackers' continued to rove."[9]

On Tuesday evening, July 30, about five o'clock, Captain John Coons with two companies of the Fourteenth Indiana Infantry Regiment, about eighty men, and a detachment of Bracken's Indiana Cavalry started from Cheat Mountain Summit on a scout in the direction of Allegheny Mountain on the Staunton-Parkersburg Turnpike.

A member of the detail remembered that they descended Cheat Mountain Summit, crossed Shavers Fork of Cheat River and had soon passed the last Union outpost and then began a long descent of several miles into the Greenbrier Valley. He thought the valley was the most beautiful he had yet seen in western Virginia, very fertile with meadows of luxuriant grass and herds of fat cattle quietly grazing along the banks of the Greenbrier River, a beautiful, wide but shallow, stream running the length of the valley. Substantial farmhouses with yards filled with poultry and surrounded by fine orchards dotted the valley. Flocks of sheep on the steep

Greenbrier Valley at Camp Bartow with gun pit in foreground.

mountain pastures with their ever tinkling bells provided the
only sound that disturbed the solemn stillness of the countryside—the farmhouses were deserted—and no sound or sight of
human presence was echoed or seen during the march. At
11:00 P.M. Captain Coons threw out pickets and the detail
bivouacked at the spot where the Confederate Camp Bartow
would soon be constructed, with the troops sleeping on their
arms. At 4:00 A.M. gunfire broke out as a detachment of
Rebel cavalry drove in the Union pickets and then galloped
back toward Allegheny Mountain to give the alarm.

Coons assembled his command and cautiously advanced
some two and a half miles, in turn driving in the Confederate
pickets, after which he decided to hold his position as some
of the men prepared a dinner of veal, new potatoes, and
honey at a vacated house on the bank of a small stream.

Soon a trio of probing Federals brought in three mounted
Confederate prisoners, and while questioning them, one of
the most unusual incidents of the war took place. A light
spring wagon drawn by two horses and driven by a Confederate lieutenant bearing a white flag made its appearance from
the direction of the Rebel camp. It proved to be Lieutenant J.
S. Dorset, a Confederate officer captured at the Battle of
Rich Mountain where his company commander, William S.
Skipwith, was killed. Dorset had been granted permission to
return the body of his captain to Skipwith's home for burial
in Richmond, and true to his word, was returning as agreed
to give himself up as a prisoner, one of the courtesies of the
early chivalrous days destined to quickly disappear. The lieutenant reported the Confederates one thousand strong and
formed in line of battle inside their entrenchments just three
miles in advance of the Union position with four thousand
men encamped in the rear.

Captain Coons sent the three prisoners to the rear under a
guard of cavalry, and as he prepared to return to the fort
with the command, a large number of Confederates, dispatched by Colonel Edward Johnson, appeared in line of
battle and began deployment of their force to surround
Coons's troops. Three companies of infantry and one of cavalry were actually seen, and suspecting that more were

Eastern Top of Cheat Mountain near Slaven's Cabin where frequent ambushes took place.

deployed in the adjacent woods, the Federals moved back across the Greenbrier River—forced to leave their coveted meal to the Confederates. After crossing the stream, Coons remained in that position over an hour before resuming the hungry march back to Cheat Summit. In the little flare of skirmishing that took place, the Federals reported killing one Rebel, with no report being made by the Southerners.[10]

Some days later Lieutenants Taylor and Williams, with twenty men from Company F of the Fourteenth Indiana laid an ambush along the Staunton-Parkersburg Pike hoping to break up some of the small annoying Rebel scouting parties that were operating in the vicinity. After waiting only a short time, a "Secesh" captain came riding along armed with a sword and a shotgun, apparently full of wrath and applejack, and having in his charge a wagon and two horses, driven by a man and boy, probably with the intention of appropriating such "Yankee plunder" as he could conveniently gather. Whether the gallant captain had mistaken his road, as he later declared, or he imagined his warlike appearance, strongly re-inforced by the applejack, sufficiently fierce to strike terror into any part of the "cussed Yankees" was a point never settled unless the captain reached a never-disclosed decision later at the Union prison camp at Columbus, Ohio.[11]

Some time after arriving on the scene, General William Loring reconnoitered the strong natural mountain position of Cheat Summit and decided such an attack by way of the Staunton-Parkersburg Turnpike was impracticable. He then decided to take personal command of the force which had been ordered to rendezvous at Huntersville and attempt to "turn" the Cheat Summit Fort by driving down the Tygart's Valley to Huttonsville and cutting the Staunton-Parkersburg Pike, using the Valley Mountain pass as his base of opera-tions. Colonel William Gilham with the Twenty-first Virginia Infantry Regiment and Colonel Stephen Lee with the Sixth North Carolina Infantry Regiment had already been ordered to occupy this position.

Loring ordered General H. R. Jackson to advance his entire force of some six thousand men to the Greenbrier River on

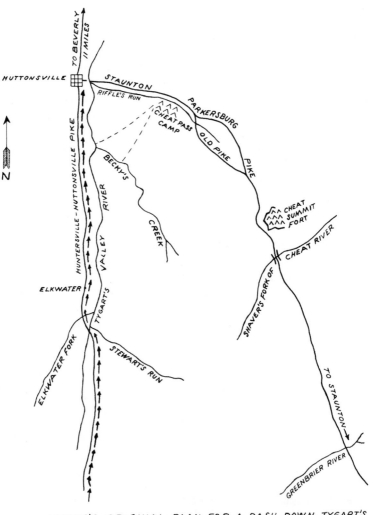

LORING'S ORIGINAL PLAN FOR A DASH DOWN TYGART'S VALLEY, CAPTURING THE ROAD JUNCTION AT HUTTONSVILLE THEREBY TURNING CHEAT SUMMIT FORT AND ISOLATING IT.

the Staunton-Parkersburg Pike, at what is now Bartow, West Virginia.

General Loring from his growing base at Huntersville had begun in a lackadaisical manner very slow and deliberate preparations for the proposed attack on the Union positions at Elkwater and Cheat Mountain Summit.

The troops then stationed at Huntersville consisted of: the First Tennessee Infantry Regiment, commanded by Colonel George Maney; the Seventh Tennessee Infantry Regiment under Colonel Robert Hatton; the Sixteenth Tennessee Infantry Regiment, Colonel John Savage; the First Virginia Battalion Regulars, Major John D. Munford; W. H. F. (Rooney) Lee's Squadron of Virginia Cavalry; and Mayre's and Stanley's Virginia Batteries of Artillery.

Colonels Gilham and Stephen Lee had arrived at Valley Mountain, eighteen miles west of Huntersville with their two regiments—Colonel Lee arriving first on or about July 31—the Forty-second Virginia Infantry and a Georgia regiment en route from Millborough to Huntersville. The effective force on the "Huntersville Line" was about 8,500 according to Jed Hotchkiss.[12]

The success of the operation depended upon the speed of its execution and speed seemed to be one of the qualities that Loring lacked, although he had a trained staff, most of them old army officers, competent to expedite military operations. Many of them were kept busy in tallying deliveries and in collecting beef, chafing all the while.[13]

The point of vantage in the advance was solidly occupied by Colonels Gilham and Stephen Lee with their two regiments of infantry, and yet to the surprise of every one, Loring lingered at Huntersville, giving his attention to establishing there a depot of supplies and to organizing a supply train, seemingly ignoring the fact that it was only a two-day march to the enemy's position at Elkwater.[14]

On July 31, 1861, General Loring wrote to General Floyd that he was making "slow preparations" confirming, personally, his unhurried rate of movement.[15]

On July 30, 1861, General Reynolds had called two scouts, Dr. W. B. Fletcher of Indiana and Leonard Clark of

Huntersville Jail where the Union scout, Fletcher, was imprisoned.

Taylor County, (West) Virginia, to his tent and informed them that the Rebels were supposed to be somewhere in the neighborhood of the Big Spring on the Huntersville road and he wanted to learn more of the situation. He ordered the two scouts to go to Huttonsville and turn south on the Huntersville Pike, riding their horses only as far as the picket post and then to proceed on foot.

Shortly after 7:00 A.M. with a little hard bread in their pockets and revolvers in their belts, the pair were in the saddle ready for a two-day scout as Reynolds had ordered them to report back the next evening. The scouts started out dressed in a conglomeration of Union, Confederate, and civilian clothing and by 5:00 P.M. they were at Mingo Flats where some women informed them that they hadn't seen any Confederates in two weeks, all of them being in camp at Huntersville. They were told that they could get lodging for the night at the Big Spring which was about four miles farther. The scouts continued on—with the sun just starting to sink below the mountain—and going about two miles, just at dark, blundered into a Rebel ambush and were captured. After awhile they were separated and Fletcher was taken to the camp of Colonel Gilham who questioned him and then passed him on to General Loring for additional interrogation; and the next day he was questioned by both Loring and Lee.

Both scouts eventually ended up in prison and were not exchanged until later in the war. After this incident, the Confederate outer security was drastically tightened and the Federals were not able to again penetrate the screen of scouts and pickets in front of the Valley Mountain and Big Spring camps.[16]

On the thirty-first of July, Colonel George D. Wagner's Fifteenth Indiana Infantry Regiment was ordered up the Tygart's Valley about seven miles above Huttonsville and at once commenced to fortify this position, known as Elkwater by the local inhabitants. The point chosen was admirably suited for defense as the valley narrowed to a width of approximately five hundred yards and spurs from the Cheat and Rich Mountain ranges jutted thickly wooded sides through the meadows, and faced each other across the stream.

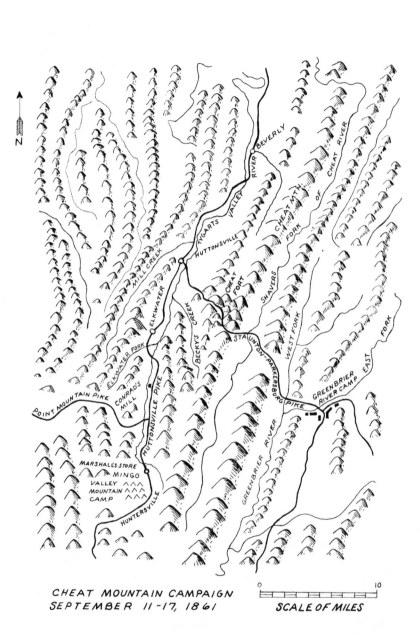

CHEAT MOUNTAIN CAMPAIGN
SEPTEMBER 11-17, 1861

SCALE OF MILES

The labor performed was almost incredible. Colonel Wagner kept one-third of his force constantly in front, scouting and reconnoitering, while the remainder worked in the trenches, or on the hillsides, felling timber for abatis—a defensive obstacle formed by felled trees with sharpened branches facing the enemy.

The outlying pickets when relieved returned to camp only to exchange their rifles for the spade or axe, thus the weary working parties were rested by relieving the weary pickets; their rest being only a change of work.[17] The situation was somewhat relieved when the Third Ohio Infantry Regiment was ordered to Elkwater on August 4, 1861, and joined in the work of scouting and fortifying to meet the expected attack.

There were snakes everywhere: rattlesnakes, copperheads, blacksnakes, and seemingly almost every variety with everybody becoming strongly snake conscious. One day one of the choppers made a sudden grab for his trouser leg; a snake was crawling up! With a fearful death grip he held the loathsome reptile tightly by the head and body, and was excited almost beyond human control. A comrade quickly leaped to his assistance and whipping out a knife, deftly slit the leg of the pantaloon—and an innocent little roll of red flannel dropped harmlessly on the ground much to the relief of the pale and fear-stricken soldier.[18]

On August 7 bearing a flag of truce, Confederate Major W. H. F. Lee and an escort of six dragoons made their way down the Huttonsville Pike toward the Elkwater Union Camp. Colonel G. D. Wagner and Colonel John Beatty rode out to meet them but were informed that the communication could only be imparted to the commanding officer, and accordingly, General J. J. Reynolds was summoned. When he arrived, it was found that the letter carried by the truce party contained a proposition to exchange prisoners captured by the Confederates at Manassas for those taken at Rich Mountain. Arrangements were made for an answer, and as Major Lee prepared to take his leave, he shook hands with Colonel Beatty and complimented him by saying that he hoped soon to have the honor of meeting him on the battlefield. Beatty

General Nathan Kimball
(Then colonel)
Fourteenth Indiana Infantry Regiment
Courtesy National Archives

assured him that it would afford him pleasure, and he would
make all reasonable efforts to gratify him—really not desiring
a fight but bound not to be excelled in the matter of knightly
courtesy.[19]

On August 8, 1861, Colonel Beatty in his Scotch-Irish
humor and thriftiness remarked: "Our fortifications are pro-
gressing slowly. If the enemy intends to attack at all, he will
probably do so before they are complete; and if he does not,
the fortifications will be of no use to us. But this is the
philosophy of a lazy man, and very similar to that of the
Irishman who did not put a roof on his cabin: when it rained
he could not, and in fair weather he did not need it."[20]

Back on Cheat Mountain, a Union scouting party, one hundred and fifty strong and composed of both infantry and
cavalry, left the Cheat Summit camp on Thursday, August 8,
1861. After capturing two prisoners, who called themselves
"Mountain Rangers," a number of rifles, and twenty-five
head of cattle, the party started back to the Cheat Summit
Fort on Friday, August 9, 1861. Five cavalrymen and one
infantry soldier were driving the cattle toward camp—far in
front of the main body which was on another road—when
they were fired upon from ambush by more Mountain
Rangers. The infantryman, one William Wilkerson, and two
cavalrymen, William Hanthorn and Harry Cheyne, fell with
the first burst of fire, all mortally wounded.[21] The three
remaining cavalrymen, unable to turn their horses out of the
road or see the hidden riflemen, fled to Cheat Fort and reported the affair to Colonel Kimball. It seems that practically
the same thing had happened the day before, except that two
men instead of three had been shot, and the news of this new
incident infuriated Colonel Kimball. He immediately left
with a party of infantry and cavalry to run down the hated
bushwhackers—retracing the steps of the returned survivors.
About four miles out of camp they met the main body of the
large Union scouting party returning on the Staunton-
Parkersburg Pike, being unaware of the shooting, as it had
occurred at the Gum Road thicket. They still held in custody
two Mountain Rangers taken prisoner the day before—near
the place of the latest attack—a sulky, dull looking pair who

Kimball proceeded to question. As he attempted to learn the number and whereabouts of the gang, they refused to answer, a right which all prisoners of war except bushwhackers were considered to have at that time. The bushwhacker was classified as an outlaw, not a soldier, and when taken was considered as a murderer apprehended in the act of attempted assassination while awaiting for a prospective victim.

Kimball, extremely angry and excited, alternately urged and threatened the prisoners until exasperated beyond his endurance. Suddenly, he drew his pistol and shot one of them! The injury was not serious but the prisoner talked freely without any further persuasion, after which his wound was immediately cared for by a surgeon.

Kimball and his party proceeded another mile or two and turned onto Gum Road where they found the three wounded men and discovered that the guerrillas had returned and shot the helpless Harry Cheyne again as he lay in the road. The injured soldiers were taken up and tenderly carried into camp where one died that night, and another in two days. Harry Cheyne lingered for two months, dying in Beverly some time after his comrades had carried him there from Cheat Summit on a litter. He often repeated that he had no hard feelings for anyone but the man who had shot him when he was down.[22] Such was guerrilla warfare in the mountains of West Virginia in the early days of the war between the states.

The scouting and deadly bushwhacking persisted and on August 16, 1861, a party composed of elements of the Twenty-fourth Ohio Infantry and the Fourteenth Indiana Infantry under the redoubtable Lieutenant Willard clashed with a detachment of Mountain Rangers, killing two and sustaining no injuries themselves.[23]

With varied fortune these skirmishes continued until Colonel Edward Johnson moved his camp to the base of the mountain (at what is now Bartow, West Virginia) and commenced to fortify that position. He made his movement at night under cover of darkness and when morning dawned the hillsides were dotted with his tents. Captain Thompson, of the Fourteenth Indiana, with his company, was on a scout when the movement was made—unbeknown to him—and

Confederate trenches and gun emplacement at Camp Bartow.

marching boldly through the valley he encountered at the base of a hill what he supposed to be a scouting party of the enemy, and boldly charged them. They fell back beyond the spur and he followed at a dead run. Turning the point, the Confederate camp, not over a mile and a half distant suddenly burst upon his surprised view. The long roll was beating and men were literally swarming from their tents. Thompson ordered his men to fall back, firing as they went, but suddenly a troop of Rebel cavalry dashed over the fields in an attempt to gain his rear, and cut him off before he could gain the bridge at the "Hanging Rock." Fortunately, he had left twelve resolute men at that point who held the bridge and ford, buying enough precious time for Captain Thompson and his command to recross the river.[24]

An interesting incident occurred in the Elkwater area on August 14, 1861, as Captain Henry E. Cunard of the Third Ohio Infantry was on an advance picket on the Brady's Gate road. Three enlisted men of his company discovered a man suspiciously making his way through the woods and halted him. Upon questioning, he professed to be a farmhand whose employer had a mountain farm not far away where he pastured cattle and had sent him after a "strayed" two-year-old steer.

His clothes were fearfully torn by brush and briers and his face and hands were badly scratched. He had taken off his boots to relieve his severely swollen feet and was carrying his footwear in his hands. Imitating the language and manners of an uneducated western Virginian, he asked the sentinel if he had "seed anything of a red steer." The sentinel had not.

After continuing the conversation for a time, he finally said: "Well, I must be a goin'; it is a gettin' late, and I am durned feared I won't get back to the farm afore night. Good day."

"Hold on!" said the sentinel. "Better go and see the captain."

"Oh, no; don't want to trouble him; it is not likely he has seed the steer, and it's a gettin' late."

"Come right along," replied the sentinel, bringing his gun

down. "The captain will not mind being troubled; in fact, I am instructed to take such men as you to him."

Captain Cunard questioned the prisoner closely, asked whom he worked for, how much he was getting a month for his services, and, finally, pointing to the long-legged military boots which he was still holding in his hands, asked how much they cost.

"Fifteen dollars," replied the prisoner.

"Fifteen dollars! Is not that rather more than a farmhand who gets but twelve dollars a month can afford to pay for boots?" inquired the captain.

"Well, the fact is, boots is a gettin' high since the war, as well as everything else."

But Captain Cunard was not satisfied. The prisoner was not well up on the character he had undertaken to play, and was told that he must go to headquarters. Finding that he was caught, he at once threw off the mask and confessed that he was Captain Julius A. DeLagnel, formerly of the regular army but now in the Confederate service. Wounded at the battle of Rich Mountain, he had been secreted at a farmhouse near Beverly until able to travel, and was now trying to get around the Union pickets and reach the Rebel Army. He had been in the mountains five days and four nights and thought—from the distance traveled—that he must be beyond all Federal pickets and out of danger. His only provisions during this time consisted of a little bag of biscuits, the remains of which were now quite moldy.

He was fed and the Union officers supplied him with clothing necessary to make him comfortable and the next day General Reynolds, an old West Point acquaintance and a close friend, came to visit him—quite a contrast in the treatment of a prisoner who was a regular soldier and that accorded the hated bushwhacker. DeLagnel was sent to the Union prison at Fort McHenry where he was later exchanged and rose to the grade of a brigadier general in the Confederate service.[25]

Confederate Captain A. C. Jones, commander of Company G, Third Arkansas Infantry Regiment, recalled a little known and rather embarrassing premature attempt to attack the

Federals and the Cheat Mountain Fort. It seems that along toward the latter part of August 1861 that Colonel Albert Rust, regimental commander, received permission to make an attack upon the Cheat Fort with his own regiment and what volunteers he could personally muster, but without cooperation from any other troops. So, with about a thousand men he set out to capture a strongly fortified position, garrisoned by three thousand men. About eight o'clock on the morning of the second day, after having covered approximately twenty-five miles over a rather easy route, the guide reported that they were close to the enemy. Pointing ahead, he said: "You have but to march up that gorge and climb that hill and you will find them just beyond."

Captain Jones remembered that for the first time he fully realized what he was up against; suddenly an awful dread seemed to come over him as his heart seemed to freeze within and it required all of his powers of self-control to proceed and set an example for his men. Looking over the green troops who seemed to be nervous and deathly pale, he proceeded up the gorge and ascended the hill, emerging upon the plateau above, only to find no enemy! By accident or intention the guide had misled them and it developed later that they found they were thirteen miles from the enemy's works, a mile farther than when they had left camp. As deathly fear turned into sudden glee; hearty laughter roared and echoed throughout the ranks.

But after the laughter had subsided, the command sheepishly straggled back to camp feeling that the least said about the whole matter would be the best for all concerned.[26]

Some of the early *fire eaters*—after a touch of war—had a much cooler appetite and a less vociferous diet. One Captain Stofer, clad in a long black coat, had made a fiery speech in Philippi—before personally engaging in any hostilities—in which he vehemently declared that he could lick all of Lincoln's soldiers with a peach tree switch.

Confederate Private John Henry Cammack of the Thirty-first Virginia Regiment recalled seeing the same Captain Stofer make an appearance in Camp Bartow after having been captured by Yankees—evidently without his peach tree

Tygart's Valley River at Camp Elkwater.

switch—and escaping after a running pursuit of many days. He still wore what was left of his long black tailed coat, but was much subdued and very docile and Cammack recalled that to his knowledge he took no further part in the war effort.

About this time Cammack's older brother Lucius was involved in a picket fight against about sixty Union infantrymen. His post was overrun and he was forced to flee to avoid capture. Being hit by Federal fire three times, he was the first man in the Thirty-first Virginia Infantry Regiment to be wounded.[27]

On August 20, a heavy rainstorm brought the Tygart's Valley River out of its banks. The Third Ohio Infantry Regiment at Elkwater had established a hospital on a small island in the river, not being familiar with the rapidity and violence of a flash flood in the mountains.

Waiting a bit too long, it was impossible to get the sick and wounded off the island. As water began to cover the high ground, horses were hooked to wagons and by driving and swimming them, help reached the hospital. The wagons were chained together and securely staked to the ground and a tent was rigged over them. The patients were transferred to the wagon beds as the water rose to the hubs of the wheels.

All the personnel tending the sick and those who helped to rig the wagons were trapped on the island. Those not finding room in the improvised hospital took to the trees for the night.

By midnight one of the teamsters, a Jacob Smith, and one of the hospital attendants—who somehow gained unnoticed access to the hospital commissary stores—had gotten very drunk. Both perched like huge birds in the trees above the rushing waters began to bombard each other with a fusillade of words.

The drunken teamster insisted that the equally drunken hospital attendant should address him as *Mr. Smith*. He proceeded to exalt the high respectability of the Smith family and declared that due to his being an honored member of such heritage that he would permit no man under the rank of major general to call him Jake. True, George McClellan some-

General John Beatty, then lieutenant colonel,
Third Ohio Volunteer Infantry Regiment.
Courtesy Library of Congress

times addressed him by his Christian name; but then George and he were Cincinnatians, old neighbors, and intimate personal friends and, of course, they took liberties with each other. This could not, under any circumstances, justify one who carried out pukes and slop buckets from a field hospital in calling him Jake or even Jacob.

Mr. Smith's lowly allusion to the hospital attendant was not received by that gentleman with much charity. He grew extremely profane and insisted that he was not only as good a man as Smith but a much better one, and he dared the long winded mule scrubber to get down off his perch and stand up to him like a man. But Jake's temper remained unruffled and along toward morning, in a voice more remarkable for strength than melody, favored all within range to a rollicking German beer song which along with daylight ended the activities.[28]

The flood had a more serious effect over in the Confederate Valley Mountain area as Private Henry Green of the Sixth North Carolina Infantry Regiment was drowned as he attempted to cross the swollen river. The violent waters washed his body far downstream into Yankee held territory where it was recovered and buried by a citizen named Ford.[29]

In the course of the many scouting expeditions and bushwhacking escapades taking place, many conflicting statements were issued and Colonel Beatty was of the opinion that the report of victories and casualties rose in direct proportion to the amount of whiskey consumed before and during the writing. Verily the pen was mightier than the sword after whiskey rations were issued.

As troop movements continued, Colonel Beatty related that on August 26, 1861, five companies of the Twenty-third Ohio Infantry Regiment were at Elkwater, the lieutenant colonel of which was his old friend Rutherford B. Hayes. Also in this regiment was a young man named William McKinley both of whom were destined to be future presidents of the United States, with Beatty, himself, later serving in the Congress.[30]

Chapter Four
Field of Forlorn Hope

With Lee taking the field personally as ranking officer in the Northwest Department it is of interest to look at some of the occurrences that had transpired during the period from April to July in 1861. A survey of these events helps to point out Lee's relationship to the state of Virginia and to the Confederacy in view of the rapid moving circumstances of the time.

On April 20, 1861, Robert E. Lee had resigned his commission in the United States Army as colonel of the First Cavalry, and on April 22, left Arlington, his home, boarded a train for Richmond and a conference with the governor of the state of Virginia. The state had not yet officially seceded from the Union, but the Virginia Convention had passed an "ordinance of secession" on April 17, 1861, subject to a vote by the people on May 23, though most Virginia officials believed ratification of secession was a mere formality.

On April 19, the convention had passed an ordinance providing for the appointment of a commander of all military and naval forces of Virginia with the rank of major general and Lee was formally appointed to this post on April 23, 1861, reporting to the governor, John Letcher. His job was the mobilization of the military forces, facilities, and resources of the state plus the direction of all troop operations.

On April 25, 1861, the Virginia Convention, anticipating the future, had in secret session adopted a pact for temporary union with the Confederacy.[1] The pact provided for permanent union if the "secession ordinance" was ratified by the people at the polls on May 23, 1861. If the ordinance was disapproved, the temporary union was to be revoked. Both Virginia and the Confederacy were acting as though Virginia's secession and admission to the Confederacy was a certainty and indeed it was.

The Confederate Congress voted in the affirmative at Montgomery, Alabama, and President Jefferson Davis approved the admission of Virginia to the Confederacy on

General Robert E. Lee

May 7, 1861, sixteen days before the people were to vote on ratification.[2]

Unknown to most, the Confederacy had begun to order Confederate troops from other states into Virginia as early as April 22, 1861.[3] As these Confederate units moved into Virginia they complained that Governor Letcher nor any other Virginia officer had any control over them, creating a bit of a problem for a time. But on May 10, 1861, an order from the Confederate War Department was issued authorizing Lee to: "assume control of the forces of the Confederate States in Virginia, and assign them to such duties as you may indicate, until further orders."[4]

On May 14, 1861, Lee was made brigadier general in the Confederate Army, the highest rank then authorized, and though a general in that army he continued his Virginia duties.[5]

All went as expected on May 23, 1861, and Virginia voted overwhelmingly to secede, that is except for the counties west of the mountains who were against secession, and who were soon to form their own "loyal" government and remain within the Union eventually forming the state of West Virginia. With the ratification of the Act of Secession, military control passed from the state of Virginia to the Confederate government and it was learned that the Virginia Convention had invited the Confederacy, on April 27, 1861, to make Richmond its capital, a rather premature, but evidently realistic invitation.[6] The Provisional Confederate Congress in session at Montgomery, Alabama, on May 21, 1861, had resolved that the congress would adjourn on the next Tuesday, to meet again on the twentieth day of July at Richmond, Virginia.[7]

At the Confederacy continued its unification, Lee, on June 8, 1861, turned over the command of all of the military and naval forces of the state of Virginia to that government. When President Jefferson Davis arrived in Richmond, he made Lee his personal military adviser and the general also continued his efforts of getting green Virginia troops organized and into the field, as well as selecting sites and giving orders for construction of defenses along with numerous other tasks.

On July 21, 1861, the Battle of First Manassas or Bull Run was fought and resulted in a resounding victory for the Confederates, but the Southern forces probably would not have been capable of even fighting a battle of such magnitude, let alone winning it, except for Lee's herculean efforts in organizing, arming, and putting troops in the field. He had even selected the Bull Run Line occupied by General Beauregard.[8]

Lee wrote his wife that he had wished to take part in the battle and was mortified at his absence. As a result of the victory—due considerably to Lee's efforts—Generals Joseph E. Johnston and P. G. T. Beauregard enjoyed immediate and immense popularity and Lee was ordered to western Virginia on what he later referred to in a letter to his daughter as a "forlorn hope expedition."[9]

Jefferson Davis in writing of the assignment in 1881— twenty years after the fact—said: "General R. E. Lee, on duty at Richmond, aiding the President in the general direction on military affairs, was now ordered to proceed to western Virginia. It was hoped that, by his military skill and deserved influence over men, he would be able to retrieve the disaster we had suffered at Laurel Hill, and by combining all our forces in western Virginia on one plan of operations, to give protection to that portion of our country. Such reinforcements as could be furnished had been sent to Valley Mountain, the headquarters of General Loring. Thither General Lee promptly proceeded.[10] The duty to which he was assigned was certainly not attractive by the glory to be gained or the ease to be enjoyed, but Lee made no question as to personal preference, and, whatever were his wishes, they were subordinate to what was believed to be the public interest."[11]

Thus on the morning of July 28, 1861, Lee started from Richmond for the mountains of northwest Virginia, accompanied by two military aides, Lieutenant Colonel John Augustine Washington and Captain Walter H. Taylor, the former being the great-grandnephew of George Washington and Mount Vernon's last owner bearing the name.[12] Two servants also accompanied him, Meredith his cook, a Negro from the Lee White House plantation on the Pamunkey River, and Perry, another Negro, who had been employed at the dining room at Arlington.[13]

The general had no escort or bodyguard, no couriers or guides, and but one solitary tent constituted his headquarters. His dinner service was of tin: tin plates, tin cups, tin bowls, everything of tin and it served him until after Appomattox.[14] General Lee always believed in a minimum of baggage, and in general, officers having small staffs, thereby leaving as many men available for line duty as possible—a theory that was to be responsible for Lee having an undermanned staff most of the war.

Lee and his aides boarded the train at Richmond and going by way of Gordonsville and Charlottesville arrived at Staunton on the evening of July 28, 1861.[15]

The day after his arrival at Staunton, General Lee set out on the forty-seven-mile trip to Monterey by horseback, accompanied by his two military aides and two personal attendants. He conferred with General H. R. Jackson at his headquarters in that town and inspected the troops encamped there which included much of the remnant of General Garnett's defeated command as well as additional units which had arrived after that campaign.

One Georgia soldier remembered that Lee was riding a dapple-gray horse and that he looked every inch a soldier. He was clean shaven with the exception of a heavy iron-gray mustache and his countenance had a very paternal and kind expression as he complimented the troops for their soldierly bearing.[16]

General Henry Rootes Jackson had been one of the most able professors at the University of Georgia before the war and had repeatedly declined the presidency of that institution. A lover of art and literature, Jackson had graduated from Yale with high honors in 1839 and was admitted to the bar at Columbus, Georgia, in 1840. In 1843, he was appointed United States district attorney and upon the occurrence of the Mexican War was elected colonel of the First Georgia Regiment and served in 1846-47. Other offices he

General H. R. Jackson
Commanding Monterey Division, Army of the Northwest.
Courtesy Library of Congress

had held included: judge of the Superior Court of Georgia and United States minister to Austria.

He resigned as judge of the Confederate courts in Georgia in 1861 to accept the rank of brigadier general in the Confederate States Army and had reached the field of operations to which he had been assigned just about the time of the defeat and death of General Robert S. Garnett at Corrick's Ford and thus gathered together at Monterey his disorganized forces as they straggled in to that point.[17]

After spending a day, General Lee and his party moved from Monterey to Huntersville, the site of General Loring's headquarters, arriving on August 3, 1861. The town was described by one Confederate as: "a most wretched and filthy town in those days, where there were many sick soldiers in a meeting-house, in public and private buildings and in tents."[18]

This opinion wasn't shared by all the Southern troops as First Lieutenant George Mills related that their camp at Huntersville would long be remembered by their survivors as one of the best camping places they had ever seen. He remembered a sugar maple orchard on a clear stream of cold water, whose banks were fringed with mint, and induced the company commander to suggest that: "Here is water, here is the mint and if some one can furnish the sugar and the spirits we'll have the best mint julep you ever tasted." The ingredients were soon secured, and in a fence corner, out of sight of the strict disciplinarian, Colonel Stephen Lee, the mixture was concocted and consumed in an undercover but much enjoyed maneuver.[19]

The day after arriving at Huntersville, Lee wrote his wife a most informative letter concerning military affairs which showed his excellent grasp of the situation. He also had thoughts of the past when he was in the United States service during happier times when the Union was intact. Doubtlessly the struggle he had undergone when reaching his decision to resign his commission and stand by his state was still very fresh in his mind as he penned the letter:

Fields of Huntersville, West Virginia. Site of Confederate camp.

HUNTERSVILLE, August 4, 1861.

I reached here yesterday, dearest Mary, to visit this portion of the army, The day after my arrival at Staunton, I set off for Monterey, where the army of General Garnett's command is stationed. Two regiments and a field-battery occupy the Alleghany Mountains in advance, about thirty miles, and this division guards the road to Staunton. The division here guards the road leading by the Warm Springs to Milboro and Covington. Two regiments are advanced about twenty-eight miles to Middle Mountain. Fitzhugh [Major W. H. F. Lee, General Lee's second son] with his squadron is between that point and this.[20]

I understand he is well. South of here again is another column of our enemies, making their way up the Kanawha Valley, and from General Wise's report, are not far from Lewisburgh. Their object seems to be to get possession of the Virginia Central Railroad and the Virginia and Tennessee Railroad. By the first they can approach Richmond; by the last interrupt our reinforcements from the South. The points from which we can be attacked are numerous, and their means are unlimited. So we must always be on the alert. My uneasiness on these points brought me out here. It is so difficult to get our people, unaccustomed to the necessities of war, to comprehend and promptly execute the measures required for the occasion. General Jackson of Georgia commands on the Monterey line, General Loring on this line, and General Wise, supported by General Floyd, on the Kanawha line. The soldiers everywhere are sick. The measles are prevalent throughout the whole army, and you know that desease leaves unpleasant results, attacks on the lungs, typhoid, etc., especially in camp, where accommodations for the sick are poor. I travelled from Staunton on horseback. A part of the road, as far as Buffalo Gap, I passed over in the summer of 1840, on my return to St. Louis, after bringing you home. If any one had then told me that the next time I travelled that road would have been on my present errand, I should have supposed him insane. I enjoyed the mountains, as I rode along. The views are magnificent—the valleys so beautiful, the scenery so peaceful. What a glorious world Almighty God has given us. How thankless and ungrateful we are, and how we labour to mar his gifts. I hope you received my letters from Richmond. Give love to daughter and Mildred. I did not see Rob as I passed through Charlottesville, He was at the University and I could not stop.

(R. E. Lee)[21]

It would seem that General Lee, himself, played at least some part in his assignment as he stated in his letter: "My uneasiness on these points brought me out here."

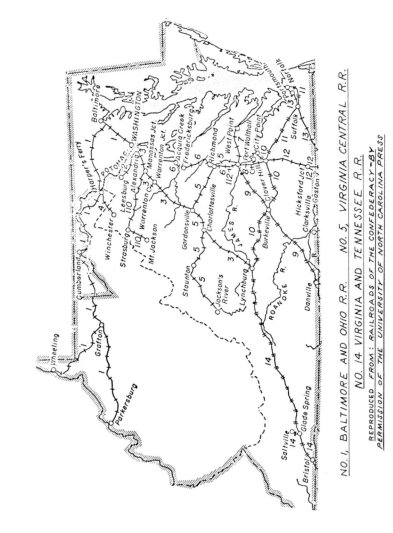

NO. 1, BALTIMORE AND OHIO R.R.   NO. 5, VIRGINIA CENTRAL R.R.

NO. 14 VIRGINIA AND TENNESSEE R.R.

REPRODUCED FROM: RAILROADS OF THE CONFEDERACY—BY
PERMISSION OF THE UNIVERSITY OF NORTH CAROLINA PRESS

Captain Walter H. Taylor, Lee's aide-de-camp said that:
". . . General Lee was dispatched to the scene of operations
in that department to reconcile the differences between
Brigadier-Generals Floyd and Wise, and to aid Brigadier General
eral Loring in the reorganization and recruiting of the shat-
tered forces of Garnett, so that, with the aid of the reinforcements sent, the army there collected might be put in such
condition as to prevent any aggressive movement of the enemy, and, if circumstances justified it, to take the offensive."[22]

Chapter Five
Commander or Coordinator

The Confederate president, Jefferson Davis, issued no written orders and seemingly did not give Lee the proper authority to go along with his responsibility or failed to make his assignment and status clear. Lee acted as though he believed his orders put him in the position of a "coordinator" and this was probably correct, but it greatly hampered his work in western Virginia. The Confederacy in this early stage of the war seemed intent on keeping all its generals with their various personalities, ambitions, and semi-independent commands happy and in one accord, an impossibility, and a very costly approach, they later discovered to their sorrow.

A hint as to the nature of Lee's mission may be revealed in Present Davis's letter to General Joseph E. Johnston, August 1, 1861, in which Davis says: ". . . General Lee has gone to western Virginia, and I hope may be able to strike a decisive blow at the enemy in that quarter; or, failing in that, will be able to organize and post our troops so as to check the enemy, after which he will return to this place."[1]

General Samuel Cooper's letter to Lee, September 4, 1861, throws a further glimmer of light upon the character of his assignment, as Cooper states: "Your several communications were duly submitted to the President, who has read them with much satisfaction and fully approves of all you have done. He has not ceased to feel an anxious desire for your return to this city to resume your former duties, even while satisfied of the importance of your presence in western Virginia so long as might be necessary to carry out the ends set forth in your communications. Whenever, in your judgment, circumstances will justify it, you will consider yourself authorized to return."[2]

The *Richmond Examiner* on July 31, 1861, may have come rather near to the official truth when it reported General Lee as being on: ". . . a tour to the West, looking after the commands of Generals Loring and Wise. . . . His visit is understood to be one of inspection, and consultation on the plan of campaign."

On the other hand we find Lee, in special orders issued on September 14, 1861, referring to himself as the "commanding general" and signing in the same manner.[3] In an organizational chart in the *Official Records* he is also listed as the "Commanding General of the Army of the Northwest."[4]

With the evidence available it is difficult to determine the exact nature of his assignment and his understanding of it. It is interesting to note that on his next assignment, which was to South Carolina, he asked President Davis to clarify his status and Davis later wrote that he didn't believe General Lee knew what his official status was in the Confederate service.[5]

Lee remained at Huntersville for a few days conferring with General Loring and urging him, in his courteous manner, to advance on the enemy and attack him as soon as possible. But it must be remembered that Lee's letter to Loring on July 20, 1861, stated that: "A union of all forces in the West can thus be effected for a decisive blow, and, when in your judgment proper, it will be made." Loring probably felt that the prerogative of dating the attack was still within his jurisdiction.

Major A. L. Long, who was Loring's chief of artillery and later Lee's military secretary and finally artillery commander of the Army of Northern Virginia's Second Corps, said that: "The arrival of Lee at Huntersville as commander of the department took Loring by surprise. Having been his superior in rank in the old army, he could not suppress a feeling of jealousy. . . . After remaining several days at Huntersville without gaining any positive information from Loring in regard to the time of his probable advance, he proceeded to join Colonel Gilham at Valley Mountain."[6]

With the distinct understanding that he had complete authority at his disposal, Lee might have handled the situation differently, but not suceeding in interesting General Loring in a rapid movement against the enemy and not having available the information he desired concerning the Union force in the Tygart's Valley, he moved forward twenty-eight miles, leav-

Confederate trenches at Huntersville, West Virginia.

Lee's Valley Mountain campsite.

ing Huntersville on August 6, 1861, and arriving at Gilham's camp on Valley Mountain the same day. Gilham's command had been there for about a week and Lee immediately established his headquarters at that position. Major W. H. F. (Rooney) Lee, his son, accompanied him with his battalion of cavalry and was immediately put on outpost and scouting duty.[7]

The Sixth North Carolina Volunteers got their first look at General Lee at Valley Mountain and were tremendously impressed. One veteran said: "It is impossible to describe the effect upon the troops upon his appearance among them. Our courage, already full and determined, breathed a new life, for we saw in him a leader in whom were met and blended those elements that would illustrate all that was meant by 'our cause and our strife.' His person was the finest we had ever seen. There was only a bold hint of silver in his hair. His eye, lustrous and clear as a mountain brooklet, seemed in its normal line of vision never to fall below the distant horizon, and yet our souls were pierced by the mingled pathos and nobility of his look. He was the most magnificent horseman we had ever seen; the most perfect citizen-soldier and the manliest man. The General had his field-glass and was making a survey of the surrounding country, when a member of the Sixth, a shrewd, inimitable fellow, stepped up to him and, paying the usual homage, promptly asked him for a chew of tobacco. General Lee as promptly turned to a member of his staff, who supplied the much coveted quid. The heart of our great chief responded as quickly to the humble private who sought a chew of tobacco as to the brilliant subaltern who sought a promotion."[8]

The General wrote a newsy letter to his wife concerning his new location and existing conditions there, with strong overtones of Lee in the role of husband and father being evident:

> CAMP AT VALLEY MOUNTAIN, August 9, 1861.
> I have been here, dear Mary, three days, coming from Monterey to Huntersville and thence here. We are on the dividing ridge looking north down the Tygart's River Valley, whose waters flow into the Monongahela and South towards the Elk River and

Greenbrier, flowing into the Kanawha. In the valley north of us lie Huttonsville and Beverly, occupied by our invaders, and the Rich Mountains west, the scene of our former disaster, and the Cheat Mountains east, their present stronghold, are in full view.

The mountains are beautiful, fertile to the tops, covered with the richest sward of bluegrass and white clover, the inclosed fields waving with the natural growth of timothy. The habitations are few and population sparse. This is a magnificent grazing country, and all it needs is labour to clear the mountain-sides of its great growth of timber. There surely is no lack of moisture at this time. It has rained, I believe, some portion of every day since I left Staunton. Now it is pouring, and the wind, having veered around to every point of the compass, has settled down to the northeast. What that portends in these regions I do not know. Colonel Washington, Captain Taylor, and myself are in one tent, which as yet protects us. I have enjoyed the company of Fitzhugh since I have been here. He is very well and very active, and as yet the war has not reduced him much. He dined with me yesterday and preserves his fine appetite. Today he is out reconnoitering and has the full benefit of this rain. I fear he is without his overcoat, as I do not recollect seeing it on his saddle. I told you he had been promoted to a major in cavalry, and is the commanding cavalry officer on this line at present. He is as sanguine, cheerful, and hearty as ever. I sent him some corn-meal this morning and he sent me some butter—a mutual interchange of good things. There are but few of your acquaintances in this army. I find here in the ranks of one company Henry Tiffany. The company is composed principally of Baltimoreans—George Lemmon and Douglas Mercer are in it. It is a very fine company, well drilled and well instructed. I find that our old friend, J. J. Reynolds, of West Point memory, is in command of the troops immediately in front of us. He is a brigadier-general. You may recollect him as the Assistant Professor of Philosophy, and lived in the cottage beyond the west gate, with his little, pale-faced wife a great friend of Lawrence and Markie. He resigned on being relieved from West Point, and was made professor of some college in the West. Fitzhugh was the bearer of a flag the other day, and he recognized him. He was very polite and made kind inquiries of us all. I am told they feel very safe and are very confident of success. Their numbers are said to be large, ranging from 12,000 to 30,000, but it is impossible for me to get correct information either as to their strength or position. Our citizens beyond this are all on their side. Our movements seem to be rapidly communicated to them, while theirs come to us slowly and indistinctly. I have two regiments here, with others coming up. I think we shall shut up this road to the Central Railroad which they strongly threaten. Our supplies come up slowly. We have plenty of beef and can get some bread. I

View from Valley Mountain camp looking down on Tygart's Valley.

General W. H. F. (Rooney) Lee, then major, commanding cavalry,
Huntersville Division, Army of the Northwest.

Courtesy Library of Congress

hope you are well and are content. I have heard nothing of you or
the children since I left Richmond. You must write there. . . . The
men are suffering from the measles, etc., as elsewhere, but are
cheerful and light-hearted. The atmosphere, when it is not raining, is delightful. . . . I want to see you all very much, but I know
not when that can be. May God guard and protect you all. In Him
alone is our hope. Send word to Miss Lou Washington that her
father is sitting on his blanket sewing the strap on his haversack. I
think she ought to be here to do it.

Always yours,

R. E. LEE.[9]

It must have been a bit embarrassing for Loring to have the
commanding officer twenty-eight miles closer the front lines
and personally reconnoitering; just how much this may have
affected his decision, if any, is not known but nevertheless,
he joined Lee at Valley Mountain on August 12, 1861.

As Loring was in immediate personal command of the
troops both on the "Monterey Line" and the "Huntersville
Line" he also proceeded to gather information concerning
the field of operation. He continued to bring his men to the
front and gather supplies for an attack, but his hesitating
disposition led to delays for one purpose or another, and he
was completely baffled by the prevailing conditions of the
weather.[10]

While Lee never assumed personal command of the army,
it was understood by Loring that he was subject to his orders,
but the knowledge didn't seem to hurry him.[11]

On August 31, 1861, Lee was confirmed as a full general in
the regular army of the Confederate States. This had been
authorized by congress on May 16, 1861, but now the rank
was officially conferred. Five brigadiers were promoted to
full general with their commissions so dated as to rank in the
following order: Samuel Cooper, the adjutant general, Albert
Sidney Johnston, Robert E. Lee, Joseph E. Johnston, and P.
G. T. Beauregard.[12]

This confirmation from brigadier to full general may have
induced Loring with all his former army training in discipline
and protocol to be a bit more cooperative with Lee.

The two areas of military activity varied somewhat topo-
graphically. The Cheat Mountain region in front of the

Monterey Line was covered by a vast and dense forest of large evergreen trees and reached an altitude of well over 4,000 feet in places. It was a damp and chilly region having a large rainfall and during this particular season the precipitation was much heavier than usual, with the months of July and August bringing a steady downpour of rain, with intervals of heavy mists.

The Valley Mountain locality, the forward staging area of the Huntersville Line was of a different nature, being hardwood forest and farmland with fine grazing for raising prime beef cattle, rather than the dense evergreen that literally buried Cheat Mountain. It was somewhat easier to move troops in the Valley Mountain country, but the rain had made such movements almost impossible in both regions.

Chapter Six
Costly Courtesy

General Lee had been distinguished in the Mexican War as a reconnoitering officer, and General Scott had been mainly indebted to his bold reconnaissances for the brilliant success of his Mexican campaign. Rank and age had not impaired the qualities that had formerly rendered him so distinguished, and Lee began to gather information by personal reconnaissances and the use of scouts, as to the condition of affairs in the Union Army in his and General H. R. Jackson's front as well as the surrounding territory.

Lee and his aides spent long hours looking for an unguarded path or little known trail to the rear of the Cheat Mountain Fort, there not being a day when it was possible for him to be out that the general, with either Colonel Washington or Captain Taylor, might not be seen crossing the mountains, climbing over rocks and crags, to get a view of the Federal position. Ever mindful of the safety of his men, he would never spare himself toil or fatigue when seeking the means to prevent unnecessary loss of life.

One day, Captain Preston, adjutant of the Forty-eighth Virginia Infantry Regiment, being on picket duty saw three men on an elevated point about half a mile in advance of the picket line and believing them to be Federals, asked his colonel to let him capture them. Permission being obtained, he selected two men from a number of volunteers who had offered to accompany him, and set forth to capture the Union scouts. Working his way through the brushwood and over the rocks, he suddenly burst upon the unsuspecting trio, and lo! to his amazement, General Lee stood before him.[1]

Other than Lee's personal reconnaissances, General Loring had to rely upon his scouts and a few citizens of that country, who acted in a volunteer capacity as guides, for all information as to the roads, the movements, and positions of the enemy. One of these citizen volunteers, a professional surveyor, having been informed that General Lee was particularly anxious to obtain accurate information of the nature

and extent of the works of the Union fort on Cheat Mountain Summit, undertook the task of reaching such a place on
the mountain that would enable him to take a deliberate and
careful study of the fortified position. He was also to ascer-
tain and report if it was practicable to lead a body of infantry
to the vicinity of that place by a route which could be used
to conceal the movement of the troops.

The only way other than the turnpike by which such a
point could be reached was by locating a route up and down
the steep and rugged sides of the mountains, through the
thick undergrowth and trees and over and around the great
boulders, traveling completely by compass, stars, and in-
stinct.

The civilian engineer made the trip successfully, located
the camp and obtained a complete view of the Union works.
On a second reconnaissance he was accompanied by Colonel
Albert Rust of the Third Arkansas Infantry Regiment, who
was very enterprising and anxious to make a personal observation. Together they made the rugged trip, and again
complete success crowned their effort. A panorama of the
entire line of works occupied by the Federals was viewed
without discovery.

Early in September, General Jackson reported to General
Loring that Colonel Rust had made the reconnaissance, and
had discovered a route, though difficult, by which infantry
could be moved.

In the meantime another route was discovered, leading
along the western side of Cheat Mountain, by which troops
could be conducted to a point on the Staunton-Parkersburg
Turnpike about two miles in the rear of the Federal works at
the Summit.[2]

Soon after, Colonel Rust reported in person to General
Lee, and described the works as such that could be taken if
attacked from the direction of the point reached by them,
from which they could plainly see all that was going on
within; and on which flank the enemy appeared to have be-
stowed but little attention. The only difficulty was to reach
this point with a body of troops without attracting the attention of the enemy and losing the important element of sur-

prise. Of the successful accomplishment of this, however, Colonel Rust was very confident, and enthusiastically asked to be permitted to personally lead a column in an assault upon the Cheat Summit Fort.[3]

Lee, in his courteous manner, agreed to Colonel Rust's request in *what was to prove the most costly and the most critical decision of the entire campaign.*

Colonel Garnett Andrews, who was a lieutenant of infantry at the time and detailed to act as General H. R. Jackson's assistant adjutant general during the campaign, remembered that Lee's first plan was to attack the Union position at Elkwater with both the divisions of Jackson and Loring driving down the Valley road. He said that Loring became convinced of the merit of Rust's discovery and urged Lee to change his plan to a multi-column attack with Jackson attacking the front of the Cheat Summit Fort and Rust falling upon the rear, while Loring, himself, assaulted the Elkwater position. He recalled that Lee yielded with reluctance, but finally changed his plan, and after some interchange of dispatches by special couriers, adopted the idea.[4]

Rust was a giant of a man with an ebony black beard, very impressive in his physical appearance and quite persuasive in speech and action. He had been one of the leading men of Arkansas during the days of political strife that preceded the great Civil War. He had ably defended the cause of the South in the Congress as one of the representatives of his state. He was a man of great mental ability and fine attainments; but at least one of his company commanders, Captain A. C. Jones, thought that he was not a good soldier, too impatient of restraint, and that he never learned the lesson that the first quality of a soldier is to obey orders unquestioned. Jones recognized many good qualities but thought his principal fault was his domineering disposition, but even with this it was impossible not to admire his magnificent courage. He was absolutely without fear, always at the point of danger. Even with his roughness, he had a kind heart and was seen often to share equally with the private soldiers in their hardships, many times on a long march he would dismount and give his horse to a sick or disabled soldier.[5]

General Albert Rust, then colonel,
Third Arkansas Infantry Regiment.

Courtesy Library of Congress

He had been among the first to take up arms, raised a regiment and was elected colonel of the Third Arkansas Infantry Regiment, but he was not a military man and knew little or nothing of the very highly skilled art of reconnaissance. He was probably incapable of rendering a military verdict on whether the Cheat Mountain Fort was vulnerable from the point he had reached or elsewhere, or if troops could successfully be moved there and be in condition to fight on arrival.

Trained officers were available, West Point graduates, and men with combat experience could have been chosen to lead the column, rather than the untrained, unqualified, though willing and anxious colonel of the Third Arkansas Regiment.

Probably Lee's decision to let Rust lead the column as well as his "easy dealings" with General Loring is best seen through the pen of Douglass Southall Freeman who undoubtedly captured more of the "inner man" that made up the personality of Robert E. Lee than any other writer. In a most memorable passage concerning his attitude toward Loring but also applicable to his being unable to refuse the request of Rust, he writes: "Lee's alternatives were plain: he must wait on Loring, smooth down his ruffled feathers, win his confidence, and coax him into action, when and if he could; or else he must disregard Loring's jealousy, overrule his authority, and by virtue of his superior rank order the troops forward. Zachary Taylor would not have hesitated. Neither would Scott. Neither would Lee's hero, Washington. Had Lee employed stern military methods with Loring, as Stonewall Jackson did the following February, when he preferred charges against that officer for neglect of duty, there can be no doubt that President Davis would have sustained him, timid though the administration then was. But Lee could not bring himself to impose his will on Loring. The general was jealous; controversies were to be avoided; Lee's orders were to coordinate rather than to command; and, if Loring would not advance, some other way of worsting the enemy must be found. Instead of hurrying Loring to Valley Mountain, he set out to conciliate him and to shape a new plan of campaign in place of the one the Federals had carelessly presented and

Loring was negligently letting slip by. So Lee waited on Loring. Dealing most deferentially with his sensitive associate, he issued orders assigning troops to the 'Army of the Northwest', under Brigadier General W. W. Loring. . . . In a word, he chose the role of diplomatist instead of that of army commander and sought to abate Loring's jealousy by magnifying that officer's authority.

"All his life Lee had lived with gentle people, where kindly sentiments and consideration for the feeling of others were part of *noblesse oblige.* In that atmosphere he was expansive, cheerful, buoyant even, no matter what happened. During the Mexican campaigns, though his sympathies had been with General Scott, he had largely kept himself apart from the contention and had been a peacemaker. Now that he encountered surliness and jealousy, it repelled him, embarassed him, and well-nigh bewildered him. Detesting a quarrel as undignified and unworthy of a gentleman, he showed himself willing, in this new state of affairs, to go to almost any length, within the bounds of honor, to avoid a clash. In others this might have been a virtue, in him it was a positive weakness, the first serious weakness he had ever displayed as a soldier. It was a weakness that was to be apparent more than once and had to be combated, deliberately or subconsciously. His personal humility and his exaggerated sense of his obligations as a man and a Christian were to make him submit to a certain measure of intellectual bullying by those of his associates who were sour and self-opinionated. The more inconsiderate such people were of him, the more considerate he was of them, and the more forbearant, up to the point where his patience failed and his temper broke bounds. Then he would freeze men quickly in the cold depths of his wrath. Prior to this time no man, probably, had guessed it of him, and doubtless he was unconscious of this weakness; but from those days at Huntersville until Longstreet was wounded in the Wilderness on May 6, 1864, there always was a question whether Lee, in any given situation, would conquer his inordinate amiability or would permit his campaigns to be marred or his battles to be lost by it. Of some other commanders in the great American tragedy one might have to ask whether they were drunk or sober on a given day, whether they were indolent or aggressive, whether they lost their heads in the emergency or mastered themselves. Of Lee it became necessary to ask, for two years and more, whether his judgment as a soldier or his consideration as a gentleman dominated his acts."[6]

But, it was also these same characteristics that earned Lee the great respect and loyalty that the rank and file of the Army of Northern Virginia would always have for him; and Lee, unknowingly, laid the groundwork for this respect at Valley Mountain in his treatment of the common soldier. Probably no army commander was ever accorded greater love, devotion, and confidence by an army than was Lee by his tattered, underfed, and outnumbered legions of 1861-1865.

One Confederate private recalled coming in from picket duty and kneeling to drink at a spring near General Lee's headquarters and Lee called to him not to drink there as his horse drank from it and told him to come and drink from the spring near his tent. The soldier recalled that at that time Lee did not wear a beard, but had a large, dark mustache sprinkled with a little gray and was the very picture of a magnificent general and horseman.[7] Before Lee left western Virginia he had grown a full beard which he would continue to wear for the rest of his life.

John Worsham of the Twenty-first Virginia Infantry Regiment remembered Lee at Valley Mountain and that he: ". . . pitched his headquarters tent about one or two hundred yards from our company. He soon won the affection of all by his politeness and notice of the soldiers. He very often had something to say to the men; and it soon became known that when some of the people in the neighborhood sent him something good to eat, the articles were sent to some sick soldier as soon as the messenger got out of sight. . . . He was well aware of the arduous duties we had to do at that time. On a rainy night a private . . . of our regiment was on guard duty. Soon after getting to his post he took a seat on a log, thinking he could protect himself and his gun from the rain better in this position. . . . he was approached by the corporal of the guard, who accused the man of being asleep on his post. This the man denied, stating that, the ground being so soft from the rain, he did not hear the corporal approach. The corporal arrested him, took him to the guard house, and turned him over to the officer of the guard. At that time it was considered a capital offense for a man to be caught asleep on post; the offense was punishable by death.

"In the morning the captain of the guard consulted with the officers of the regiment as to what should be done. All of them thought the private ought to be shot. Things began to look blue for the man when, as by inspiration, the captain said, 'Well, General Lee is here, and he knows, and I'll carry you to him.'

"As they approached General Lee's tent, they saw that he was alone and writing at a table. On getting to the tent the general bade them good-morning and invited them in. When they entered, the general said, 'What can I do for you, Captain.'

"The captain stated the case and added that, as the officers of the regiment did not know what to do, he had come to consult him. General Lee at once replied: 'Captain, you know the arduous duties these men have to do daily. Suppose the man who was found on his post asleep had been you, or me. What do you think should be done to him?'

"The captain replied that he had not thought of it in that way. Then General Lee turned to the man and said, 'My man, go back to your quarters, and never let it be said you were found asleep on your post.' "[8]

George Peterkin, later the first bishop of the West Virginia Episcopal Diocese, remembered General Lee coming to his tent to inquire after a comrade that he was nursing as best he could through a case of typhoid fever and recalled him as being the "very personification of dignity and grace" and never forgot the impression that he made.[9]

On occasion Lee showed that he could be politely and humorously firm to the private soldier when the situation demanded it. Once, as he was making a reconnaissance near a picket post and found the soldiers crowding about him curiously, he turned mildly on the most inquisitive of them saying: "What regiment do you belong to?"

"First Tennessee, Maury Grays," said the soldier, Walter Akin by name.

"Are you well-drilled?"

"Yes, indeed," the proud private answered.

"Take the position of a soldier."

Akin did so, "Forward march," said Lee. . . . "By the right flank, march." When Akin's solitary movements headed him for his camp, Lee added, "Double-quick, march." Akin understood; so did his comrades. Lee was troubled no more that day.[10]

Chapter Seven
Measles and Mud

The extremely cold wet weather, the muddy roads, and the sickness of the soldiers was like a gigantic plague to Lee and the Confederates.

Walter Taylor, who was destined to serve on Lee's staff until the terminal days of Appomattox, in discussing the campaign later wrote that: "In the subsequent campaigns of the Army of Northern Virginia the troops were subject to great privations and to many severe trials—in hunger often; their nakedness scarcely concealed; strength at times almost exhausted—but never did I experience the same heart-sinking emotions as when contemplating the wan faces and the emaciated forms of those hungry, sickly, shivering men of the Army at Valley Mountain! I well recall the fact that a regiment of North Carolina Volunteers, under Colonel Lee [Stephen Lee's Sixth North Carolina], that reported with one-thousand effective men, was in a short time reduced to one-third of its original strength, without ever having been under fire. Though not to the same extent, the other commands were all seriously reduced by disease. . . ."[1]

A member of the North Carolina regiment related that upon reaching Valley Mountain it commenced raining and the rich loam and limestone soil soon left the roads in terrible condition and the whole earth seemed full of water, with springs bubbling up in their tents which were of thin cloth and far from water repellent. The rain, cold and chilly, fell almost daily for weeks with only wet blankets for bedding, and when measles broke out in epidemic proportions, exposure was so unavoidable that pneumonia or typhoid fever often followed the first illness.

There were no experienced nurses, no suitable food for nourishment, and no competent cooks to prepare anything for the sick. Many times the surgeon and assistant surgeon became sick and privates were detailed from the ranks for medical service. Transportation was short and soon the mountain was converted into a sick camp, and as men began to die, a large graveyard was soon in evidence. As transportation permitted, the sick were moved to hospitals established in the rear, but many unmarked Confederate graves still dot the area and the countryside from Valley Mountain to Staunton, Virginia.[2]

Lee's great concern of the situation is reflected in a letter to his two daughters who were in Richmond as he wrote of foul weather and the poor condition of the troops, but over these troubles his extreme patience that was such a vital part of his greatness, prevailed. Lee's many virtues coincided with his constant reading of the Bible and his great faith in God and that all things fell within or outside His will and the success or failure was measured accordingly. Almost all of his letters make some mention of the will of God and of Lee's prayers for the protection for his loved ones; on such a principle was his life founded and this letter also reflects such:

> VALLEY MOUNTAIN, August 29, 1861.
> "My Precious Daughters": I have just received your letters of the 24th and am rejoiced to hear that you are well. . . . It rains here all the time, literally. There has not been sunshine enough since my arrival to dry my clothes. Perry is my washerman, and socks and towels suffer. But the worst of the rain is that the ground has become so saturated with water that the constant travel on the roads has made them almost impassable, so that I cannot get up sufficient supplies for the troops to move. It is raining now. Has been all day, last night, day before, and day before that, etc., etc. But we must be patient. It is quite cool, too. I have on all my winter clothes and am writing in my overcoat. All the clouds seem to concentrate over this ridge of mountains, and by whatever wind they are driven, give us rain. The mountains are magnificent. The sugar-maples are beginning to turn already, and the grass is luxuriant.
> Richmond [Lee's horse] has not been accustomed to such fare or such treatment. But he gets along tolerably, complains some, and has not much superfluous flesh.[3] There has been much sickness among the men—measles, etc.—and the weather has been unfavourable. I hope their attacks are nearly over, and that they will come out with the sun. Our party has kept well. . . . Although we may be too weak to break through the lines, I feel well satisfied that the enemy cannot at present reach Richmond by either of these routes, leading to Staunton, Milborough or Coving-

ton. He must find some other way. . . . God bless you, my children, and preserve you from all harm is the constant prayer of
Your devoted father,
R. E. Lee.[4]

Lee wrote the letter wearing his overcoat and it had indeed been cold; on the thirteenth of August 1861 it had snowed on Cheat Mountain and on the night of August 14-15 at Valley Mountain, ice had formed as the temperature fell and the troops had to build large fires and make many trips from their tents to warm themselves throughout the night.[5]

The private soldier saw the terrible weather conditions about the same as the general officers with perhaps a bit more humor. John Worsham of the Twenty-first Virginia Infantry wrote from the Valley Mountain camp: "I never saw so much mud. It seemed to rain every day. It got to be a saying in our company that you must not halloo loud; for if you should, we would immediately have a hard shower. When some of the men on their return picket had to shoot off their guns to get the load out, it brought on a regular flood. Granville Gray always said it rained 32 days in August. I was told by wagoners that it was hard for them to haul from Millboro (60 miles away) any more than it took to feed their teams back and forth. I saw dead mules lying in the road with nothing but their ears showing."[6] Worsham's statements are typical of the American soldier of all ages living under such conditions, and poking fun at his tormentors to ease the pressure and tension.

George Peterkin of the same regiment confirmed the awful weather conditions saying: "It was indeed a fearful summer. We camped on Valley Mountain forty-three days, and it rained thirty-seven days out of the number. Our picket duty was frequent and exhausting, and owing to the character of the country and the prevailing bad weather, without the compensations that sometimes attach to such service. I remember, however, in my own case one striking exception to this dull monotony of hard and unattractive duty, when standing on picket at the foot of this mountain, one dark and rainy night, I made a horseman dismount and advance through the mud to give the countersign, and then found to my satis-

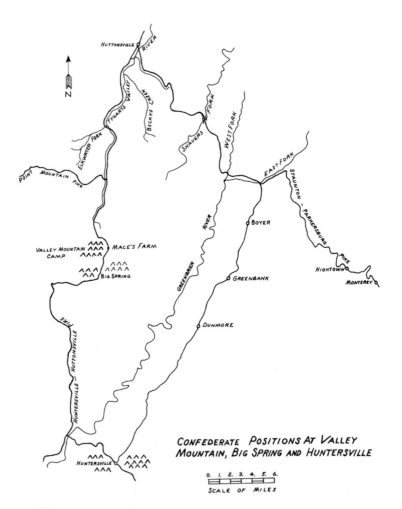

CONFEDERATE POSITIONS AT VALLEY
MOUNTAIN, BIG SPRING AND HUNTERSVILLE

0. 1. 2. 3. 4. 5. 6.
SCALE OF MILES

faction that it was Professor Gildersleeve of the University of Virginia, who had in my college days frequently held me up in the paths of Greek history and literature, by demanding countersigns of which I had no knowledge, and conditions had changed and I was holding him up."[7]

The mountain roads had become axle deep in mud, cut up by the constant traffic of the heavy army wagon trains. Passage became almost impossible and even the hard swearing army teamsters could scarcely move a wheel in the mountain mud. Many of the streams that crossed the roads had no bridges and were swollen by the constant rains, adding to the difficulties.

In the other Confederate camp on Greenbrier River things were no better. One soldier, James E. Hall, of the Thirty-first Virginia Infantry Regiment said the camp was located in the midst of rattlesnakes, Yankees, and bears, *A onme id genus* (all of a kind). Young Hall, smelling the approaching conflict wrote the following in his diary:

NOTICE!!!

Sept. 7 . . .
If I should be so unfortunate as to be slain in any battle and if any (black hearted) kind Yankee should find this on my carcass while looking for other things of far greater value, of which I have not any amount, I will be much obliged to have him to send it to Miss Emma I. Hall, Elk Creek, Barbour Co. Va. I will be much obliged to any person to do likewise, if they should find it after I lose it.

James E. Hall
Camp Bartow, Sept. 7, '61[8]

The continuous damp and chilly weather caused a great amount of sickness of every kind among the thousands of unseasoned troops, until nearly half of the army was laid up in poorly provided hospitals, and the mortality from sickness was very great. Nearly every house in the sparsely settled country was converted into a hospital, and tents filled with the sick were pitched all along the roads to the rear of the armies.

Supply trains could not reach the camps and the army was on short rations. Most of the men were not accustomed to the exposure of the elements and so fell easy victims to the diseases.

The Confederates considered the country impractical for military operations, inhospitable, and extremely dismal; and the Union troops shared the same opinion. As to the impracticability, mountain country throughout the ages has always presented difficulties for the military. As to being inhospitable, the Confederates felt the country was strongly anti-Confederate and the Federals felt that it was equally anti-Union. No doubt some of the local residents had strong feelings on the matter, some Union, some Confederate, but the great majority were simply trying to stay out of trouble with either side, figuring the best way to do this was to keep quiet and tend strictly to their own business.

Located in a section that could find either side in possession on any given day with both sides scouting and reconnoitering, plus the presence of the dreaded "bushwhacker," it seemed to most natives to dictate the policy of strict neutrality as the only practical approach to the problem. The goal of most was to get through the war with their families, homes, and property intact, and as in all civil wars, the fear of the hated "informer" was present, inducing even more silence. The see nothing, hear nothing, tell nothing attitude of the local residents made the military of both sides feel as though the inhabitants were allied against them.

Dismal it was, and with the prevailing weather conditions, it was seriously debated whether the Confederate Army could be fed where it was, and it was feared that it would have to retire to some point nearer the railroad. Double teams of horses could be seen struggling with six or eight barrels of flour with the axle scraping and leveling the roadbed, so deep was the mud.[9]

When it didn't rain, there were lighter moments and the scenery was beautiful, woods of lofty sugar maples and lynn, growth of mayapple and rhododendron added to the natural beauty and snowbirds were found building nests, hatching, and rearing their young, something most of the Confederates had never seen before.

A successful forage for apples and huckleberries usually

Big Spring today.

resulted in dumplings, with the dumpling being placed in a cloth bag and boiled—in the absence of a bag, a towel was pressed into service and worked very nicely. As the peaches and blackberries ripened, pies and puddings were made and served with maple sugar or molasses and became the Confederates' favorite bill of fare with wild grapes and chestnuts also adding to the soldiers' delight.[10]

Boxes and letters arrived at the Confederate camps and did much to lift the morale of the troops: Hams, sausages, cakes, wine, jelly, preserves, pickles, dried pears, sugar cherries, gingersnaps, chinquapins, candy, pepper sauce, sweet potatoes, ground pepper, sugar, butter, and cherry pectoral were among the cherished morsels that were received.

One Confederate stationed in one of the crisp, cool mountain camps had the audacity often common to a roguish soldier to write his father in a rather far-off state for a generous supply of brandy "in order to fight off threatening malaria." Numerous comrades declared the remedy successful as none who partook of the spirits were infected with the dreaded jungle illness in the western Virginia mountains—of course, neither did those who were without the remedy.[11]

John Worsham remembered getting a closeup view of General Loring as he was engaged in repairing some of the roads on a work detail under the direction of a corporal. Loring, who was making his rounds, dismounted and gave some instructions to the corporal. The general seated himself on a log and was soon joined by the corporal who made some remarks about the work. He then said to Loring, "General, we officers have a good time up here, don't we?"

General Loring looked at him and then asked his rank. "Corporal," he replied. The general, who was a profane man, let some "cuss words" loose at him and told him to take a spade. The dirt was still flying from the corporal's shovel as Loring rode out of sight.[12]

Regardless of all the lighter camp activity, the deeper feelings of the soldiers were brought into true focus by the passing of their comrades. One entry in the diary of the young Confederate, James Hall, echoed their sentiments as he wrote: "Today I visited the burial ground of our army.

Monument erected on Lee's Valley Mountain campsite to Confederate dead of the Twenty-first and Forty-eighth Virginia Infantry regiments.

Feelings of gloomy sadness presented themselves while view-
ing the long line of graves—a little hillock of dirt forming
their only monument. I meditate upon the desolation of a
death in such a place and under such circumstances, and also
of the grief of kind and loved friends far away in the sunny
south. I entered the house—a deserted dwelling—which was
filled with the sick. Many were rapidly failing. I saw many
there who appeared so intellectual and highly educated, who
undoubtedly were bright ornaments to the society in which
they moved, leaving the world in such a place. I involuntarily
breathed a prayer to their Creator who knows all, to be
propitiator to their souls."[13]

Finally, around the first of September the weather conditions changed and it became hot and dry with storms at
intervals, but the roads dried out enough to allow necessary
army operations and minds were turned to the task at hand.

Chapter Eight
Kanawha Conflict

Through all the rain and mud, sickness, short rations, Loring's reluctance, and the numerous other problems that stood in the way of getting the army on the move, Lee also had to contend with two feuding Confederate brigadier generals on the Kanawha Line, Henry A. Wise and John B. Floyd, both political appointees, neither having any love for the other. Being longtime political rivals, they had squared off like two gamecocks and were acting more like two parliamentarians arguing over a point of order than two generals facing a common enemy.

Probably no two generals in the service were more unsuitable to serve in the same area than these two ex-lawyers, both over military age and neither in the best of health to withstand the rigors of a difficult campaign. Like two old battle-scarred snapping turtles they probed every exposed vital spot with a constant uncanny vigil with no quarter asked. Both were former governors of Virginia, with Floyd also having been secretary of war in President Buchanan's cabinet, 1856-1860.

Union activity on the Kanawha Line during the month of August 1861 had found Federal General Jacob Cox fortifying the camp at Gauley Bridge and General Rosecrans establishing a chain of posts with a regiment at each—on a line—by which he would march from Weston, by way of Bulltown, Sutton, and Summersville to join Cox.[1]

Wise was at White Sulphur Springs, (West) Virginia, with his legion and General Floyd was at Camp Bee near Sweet Springs, (West) Virginia.

Floyd had presumptuously written President Jefferson Davis on August 1, 1861, suggesting that with a union of his command and Wise's, plus what force he could raise in western Virginia, the Federals could be immediately driven out of the state and a foray of eighty to one hundred miles made into Ohio—all from a man without military experience.[2]

Floyd's commission predated Wise's and orders had been

General Henry Wise
Courtesy Library of Congress

issued that in event of a junction of the two forces or if Floyd was in the same area of operation that he would assume overall command.

In Floyd's letter to President Davis he rapped Wise rather smartly on the knuckles, as well as various other parts of the anatomy, in reference to his military performance on the Kanawha Line. Wise adroitly tried to head off a union with Floyd by suggesting to Lee other places for Floyd to occupy that would have left Wise in independent command, but was unsuccessful and the two met on the evening of August 6, 1861.

Things lost no time in coming to a quick boil and the fur began to fly. At seven o'clock the next morning, Wise wrote Lee requesting respective fields of operation for each. Floyd wanted to attack at Gauley immediately and Wise wanted ten days or two weeks to refit his command with clothing and wagons. Lee wrote to Wise on August 8, 1861, declining his request in a very courteous manner, but suggesting that he join Floyd and take any part in the campaign that his brigade might be assigned.

On the same day of Lee's letter, Floyd again reiterated to Wise his desire of a speedy movement on the Kanawha Valley and requested the number of men, arms, ammunition, and the supplies he could furnish.

Wise answered, but told Floyd what he didn't have, and in a masterpiece of hard luck and double-talk turned the subject to "general orders" issued to him by General Lee with directions to keep General Loring informed of his movements. Then, in a minor key statement, mentioned the fact that Lee had ordered *him* to call on General Floyd to support him if necessary, leaving the impression that Wise was to report to Loring and remain independent of Floyd, which was not Lee's intention. Then without so much as a "by your leave," he announced to Floyd that he had informed Lee and Loring that he planned to attack Gauley by the Cherry Tree Bottom Road, completely ignoring Floyd's plans.

Floyd now wrote Wise and requested sabers and pistols for three hundred mounted men and a detachment of artillery with two six-pounders. Wise replied that he had no sabers or

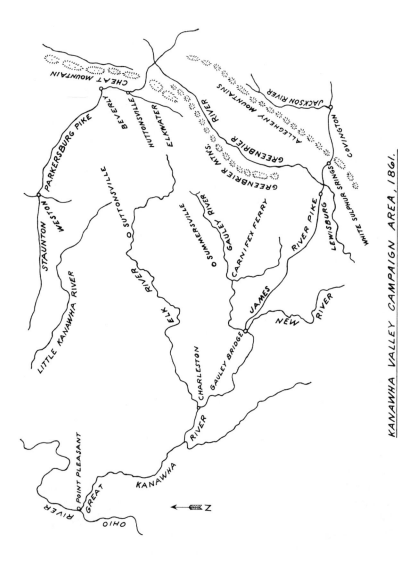

KANAWHA VALLEY CAMPAIGN AREA, 1861.

pistols available but sent Floyd a twenty-four-man detachment of the Kanawha Artillery and the two six-pounders.[3]

On August 11, 1861, Floyd issued General Orders Number 12, assuming command of the forces intended to operate against the enemy then occupying the Kanawha Valley and the country adjacent thereto.

Floyd wrote another letter to President Davis—as was his rather common practice instead of writing to General Lee, his superior—and informed him of his plans, enclosing a copy of his order assuming command and reporting great disorganization among the troops of General Wise's command, not resisting the opportunity to dig his antagonist in high places.[4]

While Wise and Floyd were feuding, General William Rosecrans, on August 13, 1861, ordered the Seventh Ohio Infantry Regiment, under Colonel E. B. Tyler, to the Gauley River about twenty miles above General Cox's camp at Gauley Bridge and where a road from Lewisburg intersected the one going up the Gauley River to Summersville.[5]

As Floyd and Wise continued their tug-of-war in words, Floyd requested from Wise a battery of artillery and such other force as he could spare. Wise answered that the request should "promptly" be compiled with, but! the artillery horses had no shoes and it was impossible to find blacksmiths, shoes, iron, or nails.

Floyd tried again, this time requesting a regiment commanded by Colonel McCausland to join him at Meadow Bluff and Wise replied that it was "respectfully impossible" as the regiment was in a state of great dilapidation and destitution, being reorganized under Colonel Tompkins. The men were without the inevitable clothing, equipment, shoes, tents, and now another item was added to Wise's long list—measles—and Floyd would hear more of these.

In his third letter written to Wise on August 13, Floyd being alarmed at Union troop movements, requested Wise to bring up his total force with all possible speed. Wise, on the same date, wrote Lee, telling him that Floyd had assumed command and had announced an adjutant and inspector general for the entire command and ordered the Wise legion to be the first command inspected.

Wise assured Lee that the legion was ready for inspection and would soon be ready for active service. He then requested Lee to issue two general orders to preserve the harmony of the two brigades; first, that no order be passed from Floyd to Wise's brigade, except through Wise himself; second, that the separate organization and command of his brigade—subject to Floyd's priority of rank and orders for service—be not interfered with. He also inquired whether the state volunteers, under Colonel Tompkins and the militia, under General Beckley, were still attached to his brigade and command, subject to General Floyd's general orders or immediately subject to his orders alone.

Lee answered Wise with another gracious letter stating: "As regards the command of your brigade, the military propriety of communicating through you all orders of its movement is so apparent, that I think no orders on the subject necessary. I have always supposed that it was the intention of the President to give a distinct organization to your Legion, and for it to be under your command, subject of course to do service under the orders of a senior officer. General Floyd, I think, understands this, and I apprehend no embarrassment on the subject. As regards the troops hitherto serving with your Legion, it is within the province of the commanding general to continue them, as hitherto, under your command, to brigade them separately, or detach them, as the good of the service may demand."

By August 14, the pot was really boiling and Floyd fired a message to Wise in the strongest possible terms, saying: "You are *peremptorily* ordered to march at once upon the receipt of this order, with your Legion and all the forces under your command." Later in the day, Floyd discovered that a cavalry company previously sent to him by Wise, lacked one small detail, his gracious rival had failed to issue them any ammunition and this little act must have just about made the day complete for Floyd.

Wise gave him little chance to mull the matter over, following with another letter saying he would move as soon as possible under the peremptory order and then had the au-

General John B. Floyd
Courtesy Library of Congress

dacity to ask Floyd to loan him wagons to make the move as he had only half enough.[6]

You can almost smell the smoke in Floyd's reply: "Sir: Your favor of yesterday informing me of the inability of your quartermaster to procure wagons, &c enough for your march, and requesting me to send you all the wagons I can spare, has been received. In reply, I have to say that I would take great pleasure in hastening your march to join me, by sending the necessary transportation were I able to do so. . . ."[7]

Wise finally ended his White Sulphur filibuster and on August 15-16 started the move to Big Sewell Mountain. About this time Floyd heard about the order Wise had issued to the officers of his legion requiring them to communicate with Floyd only through Wise. Floyd, in a countermove, revoked any orders issued by Wise to his officers that would conflict with those issued by Floyd. Wise hearing of this immediately wrote back that, "they were not revoked" and so the case of Wise versus Floyd continued, and even Lee with his magnificent calmness must have been hard put to so remain.[8]

On August 19, Wise was back on the verbal offensive with Floyd, writing him that he could detach from Wise's command the state volunteers and militia units, but that the legion would be commanded in its entirety by Wise and that he would not consent to the whole or any part of it being detached and then called on Floyd to harmoniously cooperate.[9]

On August 20, Wise made a strong demonstration in front of the Union general, Cox, at Pig Creek, about three miles up the New River but was repulsed.[10]

On August 21, Lee ordered the Twenty-second and Thirty-sixth Virginia Volunteer Infantry regiments formed into a brigade and attached to the other brigades of the Army of the Kanawha as the commanding general should determine, and the militia operating on the Kanawha Line to be subject to the orders and under the control of the commanding general of the Army of the Kanawha.[11]

Wise continued to search for legal loopholes to forestall

Floyd's orders and used more excuses to "mark time" than a small boy finds to keep from going to bed at night.

Floyd, on the other hand, made little attempt at being tactful, bluntly ordering Wise, peremptorily at times, to detach troops, guns, and horses to his own command and issuing orders to Wise's subordinates as he felt the occasion demanded, as well as ordering him to new positions when Wise felt his troops were unable to move.

On August 23, Floyd wrote to the secretary of war requesting three good regiments to replace the Wise legion, suggesting it be sent to General Lee.[12]

The next day, Wise wrote Lee that in the course of one day, Floyd had changed his orders three times and again asked to be detached from Floyd's command, urging Lee to pass his request along to the secretary of war and the president. He declared Floyd had not treated him with respect and believed that cooperation with him would be difficult and disagreeable if not impossible, and requested duties anywhere as long as it was not under Floyd's command.[13]

On August 25, there was a skirmish near Piggot's Mill on the James River-Kanawha Turnpike and the Confederate force consisting entirely of cavalry was routed. Wise protested vigorously as he had posted guards on the pike, and without notice, about 175 of Floyd's cavalry had unceremoniously relieved Wise's guards and videttes without even bothering to notify Wise.

Floyd's detachment, not being familiar with the country, was ambushed and routed in humiliating style, with some men found still running at high speed some five miles in the rear of the point of attack, according to Wise, whose cavalry had rushed to the rescue and helped to bring the action under control.[14]

On August 26, Floyd raised two flatboats which Union Colonel E. B. Tyler had sunk, crossed the Gauley River at Carnifex Ferry and surprised Tyler at Cross Lanes and routed the Seventh Ohio Infantry Regiment in an engagement referred to as "The Battle of Knives and Forks" as the Ohio Regiment had been caught in the act of eating breakfast.[15]

Floyd's original purpose had been to march on Cox's rear,

but he announced he was forced to abandon the plan because of Wise's lack of cooperation.

Lee wrote to Wise on August 27 saying that he was very much concerned at the views Wise had taken but he didn't think the consequences of being under Floyd's command would be harmful. He agreed to pass along Wise's request for separation from Floyd, to the secretary of war, but added that he thought the Army of the Kanawha was too small to be divided and hoped Wise would not push the matter, but would work in harmony to aid its efficiency.[16]

Wise continued to resist almost every order Floyd issued, and when ordered to detach troops from his command to Floyd, it seemed as though every time that he was just on the verge of being attacked himself and couldn't comply with the request.

Floyd couldn't seem to make up his mind as to what he wanted to do, changing orders several times during the course of a day on various occasions.

Both men "picked" at every opportunity. Wise had a colonel that neglected to note his rank along with his signature and Floyd demanded and received an explanation from Wise of the matter.

Wise sent an officer to pick up an artillery piece he had been expecting at the Jackson River depot and to bring it to White Sulphur Springs. Floyd, hearing of the incident and expecting guns at that point himself for his own command, promptly ordered the officer arrested, believing he had picked up the wrong gun, although Floyd's guns were also going to White Sulphur Springs. This really poured salt in Wise's already wounded and bleeding pride and one more hectic flare-up was added to those past with many more to come.[17]

Despite his many faults, Wise was a spirited and tenacious fighter and was around until the end, Lee appointing him to division command two days before Appomattox.

At one time during the Kanawha campaign when Wise was resisting a stout advance by a blue Federal line with his tattered grays, he galloped up to a young artillery lieutenant and ordered him to open fire on the approaching Yankees. The young officer protested—as the Union advance was through a dense forest in his front—that he could do no execution to their lines. "Damn the execution, sir," Wise exploded, "it's the *noise* that we want!"[18]

On September 3, 1861, Wise and General A. A. Chapman of the state militia attempted a joint attack upon General Cox at Gauley Bridge, Wise pushing in upon the turnpike while Chapman advanced from Fayette by Cotton Hill and a road to the river a little below Kanawha Falls. Wise was again met at Pig Run and driven back, and upon his repulse, Chapman also withdrew. Daily skirmishing continued and Cox was puzzled by Floyd's inaction at Carnifex Ferry. Wise had refused the assistance Floyd demanded and Lee was forced to divert his attention to this contest of wills, but accomplished little between the two strong minded ex-governors.[19]

Chapter Nine
Gentle Persuasion

On September 8, General Loring, probably on the advice of General Lee, issued General Orders Number 10, brigading the Army of the Northwest. This was designed to make the command less cumbersome and to aid in movement and handling as well as designating responsibility and forming a better chain of command.

The brigades were as follows:

FIRST BRIGADE   BRIGADIER GENERAL H. R. JACKSON
   12th Georgia Infantry Regiment—Colonel Edward Johnson
   3rd Arkansas Infantry Regiment—Colonel Albert Rust
   31st Virginia Infantry Regiment—Colonel William L. Jackson
   52nd Virginia Infantry Regiment—Colonel John B. Baldwin
   9th Virginia Infantry Battalion—Major George W. Hansborough
   Danville Virginia Artillery—Captain L. M. Shumaker
   Jackson Virginia Cavalry—Major George Jackson

SECOND BRIGADE BRIGADIER GENERAL S. R. ANDERSON
   1st Tennessee Infantry Regiment—Colonel George Maney
   7th Tennessee Infantry Regiment—Colonel Robert Hatton
   14th Tennessee Infantry Regiment—Colonel W. A. Forbes
   Hampden Artillery
   Alexander's Company of Cavalry

THIRD BRIGADE   BRIGADIER GENERAL D. S. DONELSON
   8th Tennessee Infantry Regiment—Colonel A. S. Fulton
   16th Tennessee Infantry Regiment—Colonel John S. Savage
   1st Georgia Infantry Regiment—Colonel J. N. Ramsey
   14th Georgia Infantry Regiment—Colonel A. V. Brumby
   Greenbrier Virginia Cavalry
   One Section, Hampden Artillery

FOURTH BRIGADE   COLONEL WILLIAM GILHAM
   21st Virginia Infantry Regiment—Colonel William Gilham
   6th North Carolina Infantry Regiment—Colonel Stephen Lee
   1st Battalion Confederate States Provisional Army—Major John D. Munford
   Troup Artillery

FIFTH BRIGADE   COLONEL WILLIAM B. TALIAFERRO
   23rd Virginia Infantry Regiment—Colonel William B. Taliaferro
   25th Virginia Infantry Regiment—Major A. G. Reger

37th Virginia Infantry Regiment—Colonel S. V. Fulkerson
44th Virginia Infantry Regiment—Colonel W. C. Scott
Rice's and Lee's Virginia Batteries Artillery

SIXTH BRIGADE   COLONEL JESSE S. BURKS
42nd Virginia Infantry Regiment—Colonel Jesse S. Burks
48th Virginia Infantry Regiment—Colonel J. A. Campbell
Lee's Virginia Cavalry—Major W. H. F. Lee
One Section, Troup Artillery

The six brigades were divided into the Huntersville Division and the Monterey Division with the following command arrangements:

HUNTERSVILLE DIV.   BRIG. GEN. W. W. LORING
Second Brigade . . . . Brigadier General S. R. Anderson
Third Brigade . . . . Brigadier General D. S. Donelson
Fourth Brigade . . . . Colonel William Gilham
Sixth Brigade . . . . Colonel Jesse S. Burks
MONTEREY DIV.   BRIG. GEN. H. R. JACKSON
First Brigade . . . . Colonel Rust to command Jackson's
                                First Brigade
Fifth Brigade . . . . Colonel William B. Taliaferro[1]

The Federal force in front of Loring and his Huntersville and Monterey divisions was the "First Brigade of the Army of Occupation of West Virginia" commanded by Brigadier General Joseph J. Reynolds, with headquarters at Cheat Mountain Pass.[2] The official returns for October 1861 gave this brigade, present for duty: 377 officers, 10,421 men, and 26 pieces of artillery stationed at Beverly, Elkwater and the Cheat Mountain area. This is probably a higher total than present in September 1861, the time of the campaign.

Major Theodore Lang of the Third West Virginia Infantry listed Reynold's force on or about August 15, 1861, as follows:

One Battalion, 2nd West Va. Infantry—Colonel John W. Moss
14th Indiana Infantry Regiment—Colonel Nathan Kimball
24th Ohio Infantry Regiment—Colonel Jacob Ammen
15th Indiana Infantry Regiment—Colonel G. D. Wagner
3rd Ohio Infantry Regiment—Colonel I. H. Marrow
13th Indiana Infantry Regiment—Colonel J. S. Sullivan
17th Indiana Infantry Regiment—Colonel M. S. Hascall
6th Ohio Infantry Regiment—Colonel N. L. Anderson
4th U. S. Artillery, Battery G—Captain Albion Howe
Loomis's Michigan Battery

West Virginia Battery—Captain Phillip Daum
One Company, Indiana Cavalry—Captain James R. Bracken[3]

On August 21, the Twenty-fifth Ohio Infantry Regiment under the command of Colonel James A. Jones moved into the Cheat Mountain Camp.

The preceding August 15, 1861, force probably numbered about 9,000 in all. There are no official returns for the Confederate strength, but A. L. Long, who was in a position to know, states in his *Memoirs of R. E. Lee* that Loring's force was 6,000 and Jackson's 5,000. Much sickness on both sides rendered many unable for duty and as no reports are available, it is impossible to know the number of effectives available for duty on either side.

Loring, at long last, heeded Lee's persuasion to advance, and on September 8, issued confidential orders for a simultaneous movement by the Huntersville and Monterey lines on the Union forces at the Elkwater works and the Cheat Mountain Summit Fort. The Confederates' long delay had allowed the Federals to construct excellent defensive works and to move in strong reinforcements to meet the drive. Captain Walter H. Taylor, Lee's aide-de-camp, said: ". . . the command was finally brought to a sufficiently efficient condition to induce the general [Loring] to take the offensive.[4] On the eighth of September, after full conference with Brigadier General Loring, the order of attack was prepared; it was issued, however, in the name of the latter, and prescribed in line of operations. . . ."[5] Taylor strongly hints that Lee prepared the order and tactfully issued it in the name of Loring.

The very clear and well-worded order follows:

(CONFIDENTIAL.)   HEADQUARTERS
                               Valley Mountain, September 8, 1861.
First. General H. R. Jackson, commanding Monterey Division, will detail a column of not more than 2,000 men, under Colonel Rust, to turn the enemy's position at Cheat Mountain Pass at daylight on the 12th instant, Thursday. During the night preceding the morning of the 12th instant, General Jackson having left a suitable guard for his own position, with the rest of his available force will take post on the eastern ridge of Cheat Mountain, occupy the enemy in front and co-operate in the assault of his attacking column should circumstances favor. The march of

Colonel Rust will be so regulated as to obtain his position during the same night, and at dawn of the appointed day (Thursday, 12th) he will, if possible, surprise the enemy in his trenches and carry them. Second. The pass having been carried, General Jackson, with his whole fighting force, will immediately move forward toward Huttonsville, prepared against an attack from the enemy, taking every precaution against firing upon the portion of the army operating west of Cheat Mountain, and ready to co-operate with it against the enemy in Tygart's Valley. The supply wagons of the advancing column will follow, and the reserve will occupy Cheat Mountain. Third. General Anderson's brigade will move down Tygart's Valley, following the west slope of Cheat Mountain range, concealing his movement from the enemy. On reaching Wyman's or the vicinity he will report his force unobserved, send forward intelligent officers to make sure of his further course, and during the night of the 11th (Wednesday) proceed to Staunton turnpike where it intersects the west top of Cheat Mountain, so as to arrive there as soon after daylight on the 12th (Thursday) as possible. He will make dispositions to hold the turnpike, prevent re-enforcements reaching Cheat Mountain Pass, cut the telegraph wire, and be prepared if necessary to aid in the assault of the enemy's position on the middle top of Cheat Mountain by General Jackson's division, the result of which he must await. He must particularly keep in mind that the movement of General Jackson is to surprise the enemy in their defenses. He must, therefore, not discover his movement nor advance beyond a point before Wednesday night, where he can conceal his force. Cheat Mountain Pass being carried, he will turn down the mountain and press upon the left and rear of the enemy in Tygart's Valley, either by the old or new turnpike or the Beckytown road, according to circumstances. Fourth. General Donelson's brigade will advance on the right of Tygart's Valley River, seizing the paths and avenues leading from that side to the river and driving back the enemy that might endeavor to retard the advance of the center along the turnpike or turn his right. Fifth. Such of the artillery as may not be used on the flanks will proceed along the Huttonsville turnpike, supported by Major Munford's battalion, followed by the rest of Colonel Gilham's brigade in reserve. Sixth. Colonel Burks' brigade will advance on the left of Tygart's Valley River in supporting distance to the center, and clear that side of the valley of the forces of the enemy that night obstructing the advance of the artillery. Seventh. The cavalry under Major Lee will follow, according to the nature of the ground, in rear of the left of Colonel Burks' brigade. He will watch the movements of the enemy in that quarter, give notice, and prevent if possible, any attempt to turn the left of the river, and be prepared to strike when opportunity offers. Eighth. The wagons of each brigade, properly packed and guarded, under the charge of their respective quartermasters, who will personally superintend their movements, will pursue the main turnpike under the general direction of the acting quartermaster, in rear of the army and out of cannon range of the enemy. Ninth. Commanders on both lines of operations will particularly see that their escorts wear the distinguishing badge; that both officers and men take every precaution not to fire on our own troops. This is essentially necessary, as the forces on both sides of Cheat Mountain may unite. They will also use every exertion to prevent noise and straggling from the ranks, correct quickly any confusion that may occur, and cause their commands to rapidly execute their movements when in presence of the enemy.

By command of Brigadier-General Loring:

C. L. STEVENSON
Adjutant-General

(It should be noted that the order in referring to Cheat Mountain Pass is actually indicating Cheat Mountain Summit.)[6]

The "badge" of identification that the Confederates wore was a piece of white paper or cloth tacked to the front of their hats, and at one point in the march kept Anderson's troops from firing on Donelson's column.[7]

Major Theodore F. Lang commenting on the early condition of affairs said the troops under General Reynolds had not learned the necessity of all uniforms being alike.[8] Each state or community had used its own fancy as to uniform, with the result that several of the Union regiments appeared in the gray uniforms the Confederates had adopted. So, to avoid costly and deadly confusion, identification was important.

On the next day after General Loring issued the order of march and attack to his army, General Lee issued the following order:

(Special Orders)   HEADQUARTERS OF THE FORCES
   (No. —)   Valley Mountain, Va., September 9, 1861

The forward movement announced to the Army of the Northwest in Special Order No. 28, from its headquarters, of this date, gives the general commanding the opportunity of exhorting the troops to keep steadily in view the great principles for which they contend, and to manifest to the world their determination to maintain them. The eyes of the country are upon you. The safety of your homes, and the lives of all you hold dear, depend upon your courage and exertions. Let each man resolve to be victorious, and that the right of self government, liberty and peace, shall in him find a defender. The progress of this army must be forward.

R. E. LEE,
General, Commanding.[9]

Lee in this letter speaks of forward movement and forward progress which almost precludes a battle won or the retreat of the enemy without a fight. In a letter written on September 14, 1861, after the campaign, his tenor changes quite a bit, something rather unusual for Lee, and he speaks of the campaign as a "forced reconnaissance" of the enemy's position.

As the time of battle neared some Confederate units still occupied Huntersville and Lee's so called Valley Mountain force consisted of troops both there and at Big Spring, some three miles farther south on the Huntersville-Huttonsville Pike with the Valley Mountain position approximately sixteen miles south of the Federals' Elkwater fortifications on the same road. By bridle path it was twenty miles from the Valley Mountain Camp to General H. R. Jackson's position on Greenbrier River, but it was thirty miles by wagon road between the two Confederate camps and the Staunton-Parkersburg Turnpike led from General Jackson's camp some twelve miles northwest to the Cheat Mountain Fort.

From the Union camp at Elkwater it was seven miles east by bridle path to the Cheat Summit Fort, Lee's first objective, but seventeen miles by the turnpike roads by way of Huttonsville.

In the Confederates' initial move, the troops had to be maneuvered from their various camps to allow the respective columns to arrive simultaneously and secretly at their various points of attack. Such a move was difficult to coordinate on any battlefield and much more so with the muddy roads and pathless terrain of the heavily wooded mountains.

The Federals around Elkwater and Cheat Mountain knew something was in the wind and weren't particularly cooperative with Lee's plans, making a vigorous attempt to unmask the Confederate intentions. On the very day that Loring

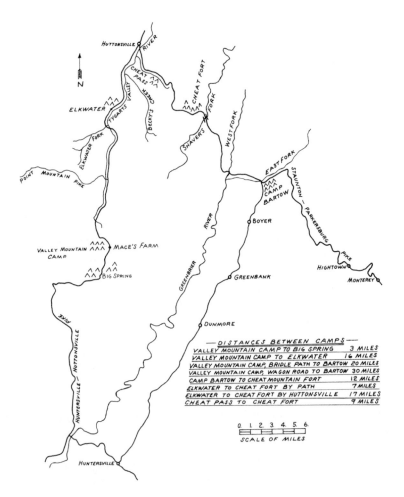

View from one of the trails from Elkwater to Cheat Mountain Pass.

issued the battle orders, Colonel George D. Wagner of the Fifteenth Indiana Infantry dispatched a strong scouting party under Lieutenant Colonel Richard Owen of that regiment and ordered him to proceed on the Huntersville-Huttonsville Pike until he met the enemy but not to bring on a general engagement. The party consisted of 285 infantrymen of the Fifteenth Indiana and Third Ohio Infantry regiments, along with four dragoons to be used as messengers.[10] They moved out of camp about noon on Sunday, under Lieutenant Colonel Owen and guided by a Dr. Singer, a Union Virginian who had practiced in the locality and was thoroughly acquainted with the area.

An advance scouting party of twenty men was thrown in front of the main body, and knowing they were in Rebel territory, the command proceeded most cautiously. They slept on their arms that night with half of the group awake at a time, having no fires, perfect silence, and crossroads picketed in their rear—as advised by the guide—to avoid a surprise by the enemy.

At 4:00 A.M. on September 9, the command was on the march towards Marshall's store (Mingo) which was very near the Confederate Valley Mountain Camp. They carefully scouted the laurel thickets which lined both sides of the road, when suddenly the Union scouts opened fire, having come so close to the Confederate pickets that a hand to hand scuffle occurred between an Indiana volunteer and a North Carolina soldier of the Confederacy. A brisk but brief skirmish followed and Lieutenant Colonel Owen ordered his command to fire by sections, to countermarch, reform, and load in the rear. With three full Confederate companies appearing and knowing that they were in strong force quite close, Owen stayed in line until the Rebel fire ceased and then retired to the main camp, 11¼ miles north, stopping long enough to care for the wounds of one of his men.[11]

Confederate prisoners subsequently told Union officers that they had lost fifteen, killed, and about as many wounded in the skirmish, but no official report was ever issued.[12]

Later, on the same day, Colonel Wagner ordered Captain William J. Templeton with D and F companies to take posses-

General George D. Wagner, then colonel, Fifteenth Indiana Infantry Regiment.
Courtesy Library of Congress

sion of and hold the Point Mountain Pike at its junction with the Huntersville-Huttonsville road, supported by Major Christopher of the Sixth Ohio Infantry Regiment with one hundred men at Conrad's Mill two miles in the rear. The forward position was eight miles in front of Colonel Wagner's Elkwater camp and four miles from the enemy's advance position. Thus were the Federal troop dispositions on September 9, 1861, on the Huntersville-Huttonsville Pike with the various side roads and other positions strongly picketed.

While Lee's main force was at Mace's farm on Valley Mountain, outpost camps stretched as far as behind Point Mountain, which the Union pickets still held and had occupied with a regiment from the time of the first Confederate forward movement. The Union route of march to this strong post was along a ravine, formed by Elkwater Fork, a turbulent mountain stream, hurrying its waters to the Tygart's Valley River. The bed of the stream, filled with boulders and shelving rocks over which the waters rapidly rushed, formed the roadbed for one-half the distance. Seven or eight miles from the mouth of the ravine was an abandoned pike leading to the summit of Point Mountain and continuing along the crest of the main spur, which intersected the Huntersville Pike. The regimental marches up this turbulent stream were usually made by the men after dark, stumbling over the rocks with much grumbling and ill-humored complaining.

On the ninth of September, Colonel M. S. Hascall's Seventeenth Indiana Infantry Regiment relieved Colonel N. L. Anderson's Sixth Ohio Regiment at Point Mountain. Hascall, before starting out, remarked that his regiment had marched hundreds of miles in western Virginia, and had always heard of the enemy in force a short distance ahead, but had never yet been able to find him. He began to doubt whether there was any considerable Rebel force in the country. It was late when the regiment arrived, the night was clear, the stars twinkled brightly, and Colonel Hascall asked where the enemy was.

Colonel Anderson, pointing to the distant hills, replied, "They are there," and directed the attention of Hascall to the smoke curling like mist above the crest of the hills.

Tygart's Valley River in the vicinity of Conrad's Mill where Captain Templeton was positioned.

Intersection of the Point Mountain Pike and Huntersville-Huttonsville Pike.

Hascall said, "I can not see it."

Anderson dryly replied, "You will see it in the morning."

The pickets were relieved but the men of the Seventeenth, like their colonel, had little faith in the report that a large army was in their front. The remembrance of their night marches to the summit of Cheat and other points for a fight and their repeated disappointments chafed them. They felt that a sortie from the enemy's camp would be a relief. This time they were not disappointed; before dawn the rumbling of wheels and the murmur of voices were heard, and when morning broke, the hillsides were still dotted with tents, the teams were passing to and fro to the mill, as was their custom, and field glasses showed sentries on post. But, the Confederate Army was on the move.[13]

Over on Cheat Mountain Colonel Kimball felt something was astir and strengthened his pickets and camp guard. He also removed the planking of the bridge across Shaver's Fork of Cheat River in front of the fort and built wings of logs as a protection for sharpshooters on each side of it.[14]

Chapter Ten
Rendezvous in the Rain

The Confederate forces had started to move to their designated positions, all to be reached no later than the night of September 11 and ready for the dawn attack on the twelfth.

Over on the Greenbrier, Rust's column was the first to move out, getting under way on September 9.[1]

General D. S. Donelson's brigade would be on the move from Valley Mountain at sunrise on the tenth, followed by Anderson's men at 9:00 A.M. on the same day.

The columns pushing directly down the Tygart's Valley would not leave until the eleventh, as would General H. R. Jackson's force later on the same day from Greenbrier River.[2]

Lee's plan called for an assaulting force of not more than 2,000 men, led by Colonel Albert Rust of the Third Arkansas Infantry Regiment in position along the Staunton-Parkersburg Turnpike, on the "middle top" of Cheat Mountain on the night of September 11, and ready to attack at dawn. Rations were drawn, orders issued, and the brigade was under way, the first of the Monterey Division to move.

Rust's route of march was to move along the Staunton Pike up the eastern top of Cheat Mountain as far as Slaven's cabin and then turn left by the paths and through the forest to the main or Shaver's Fork of Cheat River to turn the Federal right and gain its rear.[3]

The command was actually between 1,500 and 1,600 strong and consisted of the Thirty-first Virginia Infantry Regiment, Colonel W. L. Jackson; the Twenty-third Virginia Infantry Regiment, Colonel W. B. Taliaferro; the Thirty-seventh Virginia Infantry Regiment, Colonel S. V. Fulkerson; the Ninth Virginia Infantry Battalion, Major George W. Hansborough; and Rust's own Third Arkansas with Lieutenant Colonel Seth Barton in charge as Rust was commanding the brigade. Colonels Taliaferro and Fulkerson who were senior to Rust waived the question of rank and placed themselves at

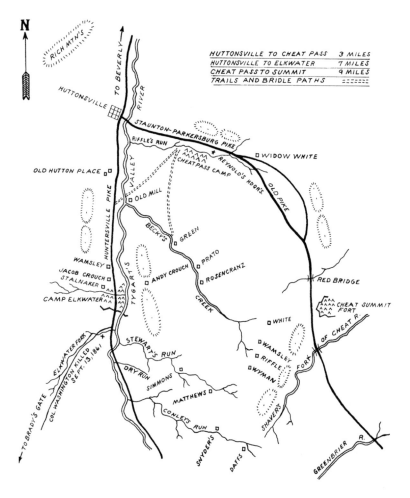

HUTTONSVILLE TO CHEAT PASS	3 MILES
HUTTONSVILLE TO ELKWATER	7 MILES
CHEAT PASS TO SUMMIT	9 MILES
TRAILS AND BRIDLE PATHS	=======

CHEAT MOUNTAIN ATTACK AREA SEPTEMBER 1861
MAP ADAPTED FROM: MILITARY ESSAYS AND RECOLLECTIONS.
THE COMMANDRY OF THE STATE OF ILLINOIS. COL. JOHN LEVERING

the head of their respective regiments under Rust's command.[4]

The column had to wade the icy waters of Shaver's Fork, for what the men probably over estimated to be as much as four or five miles—sometimes up to their chest—as the laurel was so thick along the banks they couldn't force their way through.[5] The troops were thoroughly drenched and their rations which were carried in haversacks were soon soaked and ruined. Later in the war Confederate soldiers would guard against any such eventualities by consuming all their rations when issued, considering food safer and easier to carry in their bellies than in the haversack.

At nine o'clock on September 11, the night before the attack, they were a mile and a half from their positions and every thread of clothing was soaked by the heavy downpour and river. It had rained continually since leaving Camp Bartow and it was fearfully dark, no light at all; and not a word had been spoken above a whisper for two days and two nights.

As they moved forward, each man held on to the jacket or belt of the man in front of him. Many slipped and fell, being painfully hurt, but they finally moved to within a mile of the designated position. When the order was given to halt and fall out, the men, miserably wet and cold as well as hungry, cut branches from the trees to sleep on and tried to make the best of it for the night.

Units of General Loring's Huntersville Division started to move out on the tenth of September. It was Lee's object to gain the rear of the Elkwater fortifications with Donelson's brigade by way of Tygart's Valley along Conley's Run and over the mountain to Stewart's Run, along its waters, across the ridge into a cove and down the cove along Becky's Creek. When they reached a point opposite the Federals over in Tygart's Valley, they would ascend the ridge, work their way down the other side, and fall upon the rear of the Union's Elkwater works.[6]

The Eighth and Sixteenth Tennessee Infantry of General Donelson's brigade left the Valley Mountain Camp at sunrise with a detail of two men from each company armed with axes, picks, and spades ordered out in advance of the regiments to attempt to clear a passageway for the troops. They cut trees, moved rocks and huge boulders, cut steps down the sides of the hills and mountains, and bent down small trees for the troops to hold to in ascending and descending the rugged mountainous route.[7]

Each man in the rank and file of the two regiments started out that morning equipped with an old-fashioned percussion cap smoothbore army musket weighing close to ten pounds, an old-fashion cartridge box filled with cartridges, a bayonet and scabbard, a blanket or quilt—twisted up and tied around the shoulder and neck, a canteen filled with water, and an empty haversack, making it all about thirty pounds before any soaking rain. About one o'clock the night before, orders had come to the two regiments for a detail of three men from each company to group at a certain point and cook two days' rations for the regiments and to report back at six o'clock the next morning; but due to some unknown cause, neither detail nor rations showed up, hence the empty haversacks. The rations never did catch up and the men started out with little or nothing to eat that morning. Some of the companies were lucky enough to get their bread issues and divided up with those less fortunate. The bread was composed of an inferior grade flour, and was made up without salt, lard, or shortening of any kind, cold water being the only other ingredient. The soldiers solemnly declared they had to drive pickaxes or bayonets through it and gradually work it into fragments so they could swallow it for no soldier in the army could chew it.[8]

The brigade was involved in a winding march, which the men estimated at about thirty miles, across a series of mountains and ravines that seemed impenetrable. The mountains were steep, the valleys narrow, and there was no road—not even a path.

General Donelson was ordered to keep within supporting distance of Loring's column and not knowing the country, had found a guide, Dr. Oscar Butcher, who was to prove himself both brave and efficient, rendering valuable service to the

General D. S. Donelson
Commanding Third Brigade, Huntersville Division,
Army of the Northwest.
Courtesy Library of Congress

command. Another guide, identified only as "Samuel," accompanied the Eighth Tennessee Regiment.

Proceeding a few miles from Valley Mountain, the brigade came to the top of a deep mountain gorge at the edge of an old field. Just beyond the field was the brink, and looking beyond, lofty heights could be seen across the gorge, dotted here and there with an isolated field and a lonely cottage. A few tents could be seen in the distance, but the brigade knew not if they were friend or foe. In front and below was the abyss—the descent of which must be made, followed by the climb of the towering heights immediately beyond.

The field officers had great difficulties with their horses, leading them back and forth and gradually down, as if they were following the invisible pattern of a worm fence that ran back and forth down the side of the mountain. The artillery could not be used as the route was absolutely impracticable for moving it.

The Eighth Tennessee's guide, known as Samuel, seemed to mystify all the men. One Confederate said he looked like he was just out of some dark cavern or hollow tree and was a second cousin to the ground squirrel family. Clad in an old-fashioned bee-gum hat almost as big as he was, both seemed to be relics of Revolutionary War days. Around the old hat was tied a white rag which could be seen through the dense timber and huge mountain cliffs, bobbing along like an old crippled ghost, always in front—the bellwether of the flock.

After descending one terrible, almost perpendicular mountain, the men began to wonder how the officers had gotten their horses down and it was said that the old guide, who was avowed not to be of this age or country and who possessed mysterious and bewitching powers, took the horses apart on top of the mountain and carried them down, a piece at a time, and when all were down, at his magical command each piece took its proper place, and the animals stood again ready for duty at his command of "horses come forth." The Confederate narrator conceded that the story had a few questionable points but solemnly declared that it was the best explanation he had ever been able to muster.

The men moved over the route letting themselves down by

the branches of trees or pulling themselves up as the occasion might require. In this manner, the march proceeded laboriously throughout the day, and having crossed two mountains and ascended the third, they came to the faint outline of an old road crossing a field on top of the mountain. The tired men dropped to the ground and made camp in line of battle by the roadside which skirted the edge of a woods. They had not a tent, camp kettle, or any fire, and nothing to eat, except a soldier could be found now and then with one of those "things" cooked or manufactured out of flour and cold water. The field had just been cut and many of them piled up the hay for beds and soon passed into a luxurious night's sleep.[9] Thus the brigade spent the night of September 10, 1861, on a farm owned by a man named Winnan.[10]

At daylight the next morning, the column, without food and with orders to keep absolute silence, moved cautiously along until nine o'clock when it came to a branch, then along it for another hour when it was ascertained that Federal troops had marched down just ahead of the column. The brigade had advanced faster than was intended, and was nearly six miles farther down the valley than expected. They were out of supporting distance of General Loring's column, and deemed themselves in a critical position, with the enemy in the front and the rear, and the towering mountains on either side.[11]

The cooking detail was supposed to meet the column at yet another designated point with two days' cooked rations but again they failed to show up, extending the hunger; and to add to all the discomforts, it had been raining since early morning.

By midmorning General Donelson found himself at the outposts of the Union forces on Stewart's Run.[12] Upon learning of the nearness of the pickets he immediately conferred with Colonel John Savage, regimental commander of the Sixteenth Tennessee and a trusted confidant.[13]

The pickets were stationed at the Matthew house, a small log cabin, a little distance below, and the General immediately had his advance guard moved into position and directed Colonel A. S. Fulton, regimental commander of the Eighth

Tennessee Regiment, along with the guide, Dr. Butcher, to proceed along the slope of the hill to the left of the house, thus cutting off the picket's escape. As the guard moved forward, Colonel Fulton and Dr. Butcher came down the hill and captured the pickets, four in number; thus disposing of the first post without an alarm being given.[14]

Colonel Savage with Captain Bryant's company of the Eighth Tennessee, accompanied by the guide, now proceeded as the advance guard down the valley, and soon came upon the second stand of pickets, four of whom surrendered and two of whom attempted to escape and were killed.[15] From those taken prisoner, it was learned the position of the main picket force, which consisted of a full company of infantry, was posted a short distance down the valley—at a place known as the Simmons house—where a road came into the valley across the ridge from Becky's Creek. The house was by the side of this road at the foot of the ridge and behind an angle of woods that projected into the valley. It was so situated as to be completely hidden from the approaching Confederates as well as concealing their nearness from the Federal pickets.[16]

As the two Confederate companies approached the position of the house, they came upon an armed Yankee carelessly standing in the road, and before he could decide whether they were friend or foe, he found himself captured. Just at this moment two others were seen to dash into a little brush guardhouse, seize their guns and run for the road, but they were soon overtaken and made prisoners.[17]

About two hundred fifty yards above the house three others, a captain, a lieutenant, and a private, were seen blissfully fishing. The noise of the stream prevented them from hearing the Confederates approach and Dr. Butcher and Colonel Savage dashed up and forced them to surrender, one of them being so frightened that upon being questioned told them that the whole company was at the Simmons house just below, the view still being obstructed by a cluster of trees.[18]

Colonel Savage, with his two companies, dashed upon the position furiously, and charging ahead of his force, he rushed

Colonel John Savage
In the uniform of lieutenant colonel of the Eleventh U. S. Infantry
in the war with Mexico.
Courtesy Tennessee State Library and Archives

into their very midst, and before they were scarcely aware of
his presence, he had placed himself between them and their
command and cut off their retreat. Having gained this point
so suddenly, he demanded the surrender of the whole force.
This took the Federals by surprise, and a few attempted to
make their escape, while a few attempted to fire on him from
the window of the house. Colonel Savage halted those at-
tempting to escape, and driving them back into the yard,
flourished his pistol in their faces and told them that if they
did not surrender instantly he would, "have the last d——d
one of them shot in less than five minutes!" At this instant,
the Rebel advance guard appeared, and filing on each side of
the house, confirmed the threat, and the whole company
surrendered to the colonel on the spot without the escape of
a single man to warn the Federal camp. This point was an
important one for it guarded the main approach to the Federal position on its left flank, and was also the only available
approach to Becky's Creek in the rear, which was reached by
the old road, crossing the ridge at this point. The importance
of this point being understood by the Federal commander, he
had placed a heavy picket force here to protect his flank and
rear. Colonel Savage had seen the importance of making a
prompt and speedy capture of the post without allowing anyone to escape to give the alarm as the Federals could have
brought out a heavy force in a relatively short time. By thus
capturing the post, the column could gain its position on
Becky's Creek before the Federals could realize the situation.
Fifty-six prisoners were captured and a detail was appointed
to guard them, their arms being distributed among the troops
for transportation.[19] The Federals captured were a company
of the Sixth Ohio Infantry under the command of Captain
James Bense who was one of those taken prisoner.

The rest of the brigade had come up on the double-quick,
and as the urgency of their need had been exaggerated, many
men had thrown down their knapsacks and blankets in order
to hasten their arrival. They formed in line of battle across
the valley but the trouble was over and the outpost captured.

The Federals just taken prisoners had been preparing supper
and the advance Confederates pounced upon the good crack-

ers and meat that were the Union rations and soon consumed every last bite and crumb, food by this time being the most highly prized of possessions.[20]

The column left Stewart's Run and proceeded up the ridge by way of the road and at the top of the hill a large bundle of Union dispatches were discovered in a pile of leaves in the path. The dispatches were to the commander of the picket force complaining of the carelessness of a lieutenant, and cautioning him of the danger of surprise, but obviously a bit too late. Other information was gained in reference to the position and strength of the Federals from the discovered papers. The Union courier had been unable to deliver the package to the commander of the pickets, and seeing his own escape cut off, he dropped the bundle and covered it hastily with leaves. Being uncovered as the men passed over it, it was discovered and turned over to an officer for proper disposition.

It had rained most of the day and the column moved cautiously along the ridge, and came to a valley on the upper waters of Becky's Creek. Proceeding down the run, the brigade arrived about sundown at an old house where a log heap was burning. This was evidently a picket stand, but the pickets, aware of the approach, had withdrawn.

The brigade was now in the rear of the Federal position, occupying the west base of the ridge. The Federals were fortified at the east base, and the ridge terminated on Donelson's immediate right. The general ascended the ridge about dark, and moved up carefully to the top, then over and down under cover of the night, until Fulton's regiment was within a few hundred yards of the Federals' campfires with Savage's regiment stopping at the top of the hill. The path was narrow over which the troops moved, and the undergrowth was so thick that the men could scarcely pass through it. The night was very dark, and the rain incessant. At about nine o'clock, Colonels Savage and Fulton suggested to General Donelson the desirability of returning Fulton's regiment to the top of the ridge and encamping.

Exhausted and famished, the men, many of them barefooted, stood in a huddle, easy prey for the enemy and

Cheat Mountain from Western Top.

probably not a gun could have been fired as the muskets had been thoroughly drenched by the rain for hours.

Finally the word was quietly passed along the line to "about face!" and move out. Slowly and despondently the tired men turned and struggled back up the mountain again. Without a single ration, or food of any kind, and without a tent or blanket, the Confederates testified that they spent one of the most terrible nights of the war. The darkness was so thick that the Tennesseans solemnly declared they cut it with knives and others, equally as serious, declared they tried to eat it. The winds were high that night and the rain literally flooded the mountain. Occasionally a soldier would superfluously call for "more water!" as it would wash under his sleeping position, and usually, he had his order filled immediately.

To really top things off and end a lovely day, a bear made its way into camp about midnight and really created some excitement during which the prisoners tried to escape but failed. The bear soon found that it was in an extremely poor position and hurriedly made his exit, discovering that a bear had no business among a brigade of hungry, wet, angry, Confederate soldiers. All in all, rest and sleep were scarce commodities that night for Donelson's Brigade.

As the brigades of the Huntersville Division continued to move out, General Anderson was under way at 9:00 A.M. on September 10 with orders to move along the byways and bridle paths on the western slope of Cheat Mountain, taking care to conceal his movement, both day and night, in order to get possession of the Staunton-Parkersburg Pike on the western top of Cheat Mountain in the rear of the fort. He was to be on the pike at dawn on September 12 and cut the telegraph wire connecting the Federal camps, thus breaking their line of communication; to post his men in positions to cut off any reinforcements coming from the Elkwater camp; guard against attack from the fort; and aid in the assault of Colonel Rust's column if necessary on the Cheat stronghold. He was especially to take care not to reveal the surprise movement of Rust's command; and after the opening attack, he was to try and establish contact with Rust's column. His

General S. R. Anderson
Courtesy Tennessee State Library and Archives

route was twenty miles long and very difficult. They had a most laborious task and started off with seven days' rations with the object of reaching in two days a point on the pike some three miles in the rear of the Cheat fortifications.

In order to do this, they had to fight their way through thickets and climb up and slide down the mountainsides. It was not uncommon to see a mule slide twenty feet down a slope and strong men sink down exhausted trying to get up the rugged mountainsides.[21]

Dr. Charles Quintard, Confederate chaplain, who was present on the march, said that he had reached the top of a high mountain on the first day and sat down to rest under a boulder that projected out into the pathway when an officer called to him, "Tell them the order is to double-quick!" The good doctor passed the command to another officer who turned to those who were behind him and relayed the order. The rear of the regiment turned and rushed pell-mell down the mountain, and in the process, unceremoniously upset their major, who, with heels flying high in the air, poured forth benedictions most unusual for a Presbyterian elder.

The inevitable rains came about midnight that night and one soldier said he slept in the bed of a river with a thin sheet of water over him, but most made no claim to such conveniences and luxuries.

The next morning the troops breakfasted on cold meat and "gutta-percha" bread, took up the line of march, but made slow progress, keeping perfect silence and expecting to run into Federal scouting parties at any minute.[22] At about 3:00 P.M., orders were passed along the line just as about half of the regiment had reached the top of a mountain to "double-quick forward!" Federal drums could be distinctly heard beating at some unknown location and the column moved forward as rapidly as possible, taking about an hour to descend the mountain. All horses had to be left behind as the terrain was so steep and rocky that it was impossible for them to go any farther.

One officer recalled that: "The second night out [September 11] we slept on a mountain that in soil and growth was more like a forest. Here we tried to sleep but the rain poured so, and the torrents ran down the mountain in such a flood of water that we would have drowned had we laid on the ground."[23]

Meanwhile on the morning of September 11, Lee's forward movement down the Tygart's Valley had begun by the successive marching of the columns under the personal command of General Loring.

The brigade of Colonel Burks was to advance on the left of the Tygart's Valley River in supporting distance of the center, but acting as the left wing of the valley advance. They were responsible for clearing and protecting the left flank, having the help of W. H. F. Lee's cavalry on its own flank and rear.

Any artillery not in use on the flanks was to keep on the pike, supported by Munford's battalion, and followed by the rest of Gilham's brigade in reserve. The supply trains were to follow the main road, keeping out of cannon range of the enemy.

The signal for all attacks to start was to be the firing of Colonel Rust's guns as he launched his assault at dawn on September 12, and solely upon this signal rested the fate of the entire campaign. The big Arkansas colonel alone held the key to open the battle.

The main column, accompanied by Lee and Loring on September 11, ran into Captain Templeton's advance pickets at the junction of the Huntersville-Huttonsville and Point Mountain pikes. The Confederate skirmishers opened fire and the Union pickets gradually fell back to Conrad's Mill, combating the advance all the way. Captain Templeton sent for reinforcements and Colonel Wagner immediately sent the left wing of the Fifteenth Indiana to his aid, under the command of Major G. O. Wood, with orders to hold the position. In a short while, a scout, who had been posted three miles east of Captain Templeton by Wagner, reported a column of 2,000 Confederates marching on the position by a mountain road which intersected the Huttonsville Pike in the rear of Templeton's position, and Wagner immediately sent orders for the entire force to fall back to the main camp of the regiment. The advance detachment lost: 2 men, killed; 3, wounded; and

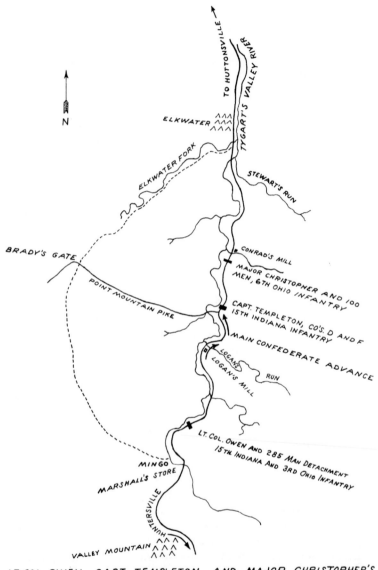

LT. COL. OWEN, CAPT. TEMPLETON, AND MAJOR CHRISTOPHER'S
SKIRMISHES WITH THE FORWARD ELEMENTS OF THE
CONFEDERATE MAIN VALLEY ADVANCE, SEPT. 9, 1861.

1 prisoner in the skirmish. No report of the Confederate casualties was made.[24] As the force falling back reached the main camp, General J. J. Reynolds arrived in person and took over the command.

Colonel Hascall and the Seventeenth Indiana escaped by the Elkwater Fork road reaching the outer works just in time. Two companies of the Seventeenth, under Captain Thompson and Lieutenant Jones, had been detached near the junction of the Point Mountain Pike and Huntersville-Huttonsville road, and there engaged part of the advance of the enemy, holding them in check. When the regiment had been ordered in with all speed, it was supposed these companies, so far in advance, were hopelessly cut off; but Lieutenant Colonel Wilder refused to return without them, and dashing ahead, found them deployed in the thickets skirmishing doggedly as they retired, and brought them safely back to camp.[25]

Over on the Greenbrier, General Jackson moved his force out on the evening and night of September 11, taking all his remaining troops except for a camp guard, and followed along the Staunton-Parkersburg Pike.

Rations issued were salt meat and hard bread. The Confederate bread issue, which never did come close to equaling the quality of the Federal "hardtack," maintained an infamous reputation with the Confederate soldiers throughout the war and really got off to a running start during the Cheat Mountain campaign.

Walter Clark, orderly sergeant of Company D, First Georgia Infantry Regiment, remembered much about the poor bread and declared he kept a Confederate biscuit for some twenty years after the war as a memento. Upon encountering an ex-Confederate of the same company, a Dr. Hitt of Augusta, he produced the aged Rebel bread and asked the old friend for an identification. The perplexed doctor examined it carefully by sight, touch, and smell, and then said very confidently: "Oh! yes, I know what it is. It is a stone from a deer's liver." Clark added that except for a sneak attack by a swarm of insects upon the old biscuit in later years, he believed that it would have been preserved indefinitely.[26]

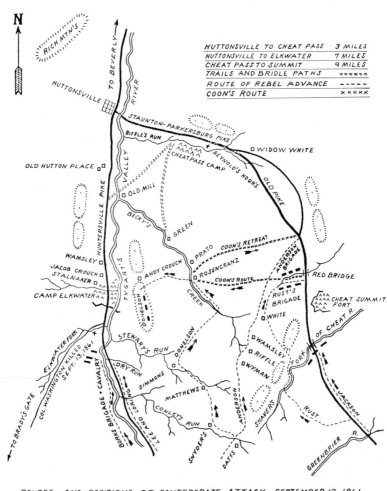

ROUTES AND POSITIONS OF CONFEDERATE ATTACK SEPTEMBER 12, 1861
MAP ADAPTED FROM: MILITARY ESSAYS AND RECOLLECTIONS.
THE COMMANDRY OF THE STATE OF ILLINOIS. COL. JOHN LEVERING

The march continued during the night and a heavy, cold rain fell making the dense dark forest even darker, and raised the icy cold waters of Shaver's Fork of Cheat River and all its tributaries. Soaked and miserable like the rest of the army, the men would, nevertheless, be in front of the Cheat Summit Fort, just on the east side of Shaver's Fork, at the appointed time ready to make a demonstration or join in the attack when Rust made his assault at dawn on the twelfth. If the attack was successful, Jackson was to leave a force to hold the captured redoubt, and with the remainder of his army, was to press on to join in the attack on the left.

Meanwhile back at the Union fort on Cheat Summit, Captain John Coons of the Fourteenth Indiana Infantry was ordered at ten o'clock on the evening of September 11 to take sixty scouts, twenty each from the Fourteenth Indiana, Twenty-fourth, and Twenty-fifth Ohio, and three dragoons of Bracken's Cavalry to proceed to the Rosencranz place on Becky's Creek. Colonel Kimball ordered him to both scout and guard the approaches from that place to the Cheat Fort as it was located on the vital path to the Elkwater camp.[27] Coons moved out on the Staunton-Parkersburg Pike, but due to the extreme darkness, was unable to locate the place where the trail turned off and was forced to spend the night there, unknowingly bivouacking within a few hundred yards of the mutually unsuspecting Confederate force of General Anderson.[28]

J. T. Pool, a member of the Fourteenth Indiana, in referring to the unsuspecting Cheat Mountain garrison on the night of September 11, 1861, said: "There lay the camp on Cheat Mountain Summit, and spread out on the slopes were the tents of *full three-thousand Union soldiers* who were at that moment under their shelter, snoring away in all the fancied security of men who expected to wake up in the morning with a whole skin and an appetite that would astonish the commissary department."[29]

Chapter Eleven
Misfires and Failures

Regardless of the many difficulties, sickness, mud, mountains, rain, the reluctant Loring, and the numerous other impediments, all the preliminary Confederate movements were executed on time. Captain Walter Taylor said: "Morning found everything just as the most confident could have hoped. . . ."[1] Each of the cooperating commands was at its appointed place on the very foggy morning of September 12, and the Union force had not discovered their movements or presence on Cheat Mountain.[2]

General Anderson was astride the Staunton-Parkersburg Pike on the western top of Cheat, had cut the telegraph after midnight—the Union operator believing a tree had fallen across it—and was in position to block any reinforcements coming from Elkwater or to aid in the assault if needed.

Colonel Rust had overcome the almost insurmountable difficulties of his march through the forest and had his command on the right of the Cheat Mountain fortress and on the road in its rear, ready for the assault.[3]

General H. R. Jackson was approaching position near Shaver's Fork of Cheat River—in the fog—in the immediate front of the fort.

General Loring, with the main body and center of the army, was within easy reach of the front of the Elkwater fortifications.[4]

General Donelson and brigade were on a ridge, above Becky's Creek, overlooking the left rear of the Elkwater camp.

All units were in position and on time and all anxiously awaited the opening fire of Rust's assault as the signal for the general attack. Dawn came and passed, but no sound was heard from Cheat Mountain.[5]

It was the practice at the Cheat Fort to start a train of wagons at break of day each morning to Huttonsville for necessary supplies and for them to return in the afternoon. The morning of September 12 was no different and three wagons of the Twenty-fifth Ohio Infantry were off early to make the daily run. After their departure one of Lieutenant Hugh Delzell's command of Bracken's Cavalry was started down the mountain with dispatches. The dragoon had proceeded a short distance—a half mile to a mile and a half—when he found the wagons standing in the road without horses or drivers and with evident marks of a struggle in the deep mud.[6]

The wagons had run into the left of Rust's command which had gained Kimball's rear and the dragoon immediately galloped back to camp and gave the alarm. Colonel Kimball reported: "Information being at once brought to me, I proceeded to the point of attack, accompanied by Colonel Gilbert, of the Twenty-fourth Ohio, and companies C [Captain Brooks] and F [Captain Williamson] of the Fourteenth Indiana. I at first supposed the attack was made by a scouting party of the enemy, and sent Captains Brooks and Williamson into the woods, deployed as skirmishers. They soon overhauled the enemy, numbering 2,500. They opened fire and informed me the enemy were there in great force. I ordered them to hold their position and soon had the pleasure of seeing the whole force of the enemy take to their heels, throwing aside guns, clothing and everything that impeded their progress."[7]

Colonel Kimball is reported to have rushed into the fray, swinging his hat high in the air and yelling at the top of his lungs, "Hurrah for Indiana, trail them boys, trail them."

On Kimball's return to camp from escorting the attacking companies, he reported with a smile and an air of confidence, "Our boys are peppering them good out there."

In the meantime, he had detailed ninety men from the Fourteenth Indiana, Twenty-fourth and Twenty-fifth Ohio under Captain David Higgins, accompanied by Lieutenants Green and Wood, to go to the relief of Captain Coons, who Kimball figured was bound to be in desperate trouble, considering the day's developments.

Kimball, aided by Lieutenant Colonel Mahan, Major Harrow, Colonel Ammen, Lieutenant Colonel Gilbert, and a major of the Twenty-fourth Ohio, immediately began to

Where Rust's column turned off the Staunton-Parkersburg Pike to flank the Cheat Summit Fort.

prepare for an attack on the fort. Colonel Jones with his Twenty-fifth Ohio, took his place inside the fort; Captain Daum with a section of Battery A, First West Virginia Light Artillery, and Lieutenant Dezell of the Bracken Cavalry assisted and in a few minutes the force was posted at all the approaches, where they lay all day.

Even the members of the bands, the teamsters, sutlers, commissary and quartermaster sergeants, and all the sick that could crawl gathered up the spare guns, forming a strong force and presenting quite a belligerent appearance.

One Indiana soldier said he could not help smiling—knowing their numbers, ability, and fortifications—when captured Confederates later told him they designed taking the fort at the point of the bayonet.[8] The prisoners also reported that the Confederate scouts had penetrated the picket and guard line during the stormy night of September 11-12, getting close enough to actually look over the breastworks.[9]

[Most, if not all accounts, other than by participants, report only three hundred men on Cheat Mountain Summit on September 12, 1861. This number has been arrived at from Colonel Nathan Kimball's report to General J. J. Reynolds, dated September 14, 1861, and the subsequent report of General Reynolds, dated September 17, 1861, and partially compiled from Kimball's report. Careful reading of Kimball's report, Official Records, Volume 5, page 187, will reveal that he speaks only of the portion of his force engaged that day, not of his complete garrison at the fort, as he says: "The aggregate of the enemy's force was near 5,500; 'ours, which engaged and repulsed them,' was less than 300."

Reynolds states: "The enemy, about 5,000 strong, now closed in on Cheat Summit, and became engaged with detachments of the Fourteenth Indiana, Twenty-fourth and Twenty-fifth Ohio, from the summit, in all only about 300, who, deployed in the woods, held in check and killed many of the enemy, who did not at any time succeed in getting sufficiently near the field redoubt to give Daum's Battery an opportunity of firing into him." Reynolds further states in his report: ". . . the small force of about 300 from the sum-

mit *engaged the enemy. . . ." Reynolds also speaks only of the force engaged, that being detachments from the Fourteenth Indiana, Twenty-fourth Ohio, and Twenty-fifth Ohio Infantry regiments. These regiments at full strength had approximately one thousand men per regiment.*

The regiments were composed of ten companies each and the reports of Reynolds, Kimball, and his reporting officers identify seven companies of the Fourteenth Indiana, four companies of the Twenty-fourth Ohio and three companies of the Twenty-fifth Ohio as being in action that day, this being almost half of the total companies of the three regiments. Also in the fort was Daum's section of West Virginia Artillery and one company of Bracken's Cavalry.

Frederick H. Dyer in his A Compendium of the War of the Rebellion *lists all three regiments as present on Cheat Mountain Summit and in action on September 12, 1861.*

J. T. Pool in his book, Under Canvas, *being a member of the Fourteenth Indiana and actually on Cheat Mountain Summit on September 12, 1861, says there were full three thousand Union soldiers present. (Compare page 130.)*

In Frank Moore's Rebellion Record, *Volume 3, D, pp. 136-37, quoting from a letter of a member of the Fourteenth Indiana states: "Under the efficient direction of Colonel Kimball who commands this post, aided by Lieutenant Colonel Mahan and Major Harrow, Colonel Ammen, Lieutenant Colonel Gilbert and Major ――― of the Twenty-fourth Ohio; Colonel Jones, with his Twenty-fifth Ohio, taking his position in the redoubt; Captain Daum, of the German Artillery Company, and Lieutenant Dezell of the Bracken Rangers; all the forces were, in a few minutes posted at all the approaches, and there they lay all day. . . ." (Compare page 119.)*

Colonel Rust of the Third Arkansas reported capturing the assistant commissary, and for one regiment *found upon his person a requisition for 930 rations.*[10]

The evidence is overwhelming that the garrison on Cheat Summit was close to three thousand Union soldiers on September 12, 1861, instead of only three hundred as reported in almost all non-witness accounts.]

Typical Cheat Mountain terrain.

In Rust's brigade, Company G of his own Third Arkansas Regiment was commanded by Captain A. C. Jones who recalled: "Day at length dawned upon the most forlorn and wretched set of human beings that ever existed in this world. It seemed impossible to make a further move, but Colonel Rust was still optimistic and indefatigable. His own powers of endurance seemed inexhaustible. He stood like a lion at bay under a tree all night, taking in the situation without a murmur. In the morning, the rain having ceased and the sun coming out, he succeeded, after almost superhuman exertions, in getting most of his men in line; but there must have been at least two hundred men left who were utterly unable to move.

"Thus we commenced our stealthy march, Colonel Rust leading the Third Arkansas, with a small squad of my men about fifty yards in advance. In about a mile the head of the column suddenly emerged upon the road. It so happened that they struck directly upon the picket post of the enemy, two men sitting quietly by the roadside eating their breakfast. Poor fellows! They seemed utterly oblivious of the fact that danger was near, and the appearance of a lot of wild men suddenly bursting upon them from the brush seemed to craze them, and instead of surrendering when called on they ran screaming up the road and were both shot dead. This firing alarmed the reserved picket, when about fifty men came down at a double quick; but soon realizing the situation, they took to the woods, followed by a scattering fire from our men.

"Of course this was the crucial moment upon which the fate of the whole expedition depended. Had it been possible to have well in hand a strong body of men at the very instant of this firing, it is barely possible that we might have made a rush and entered the works half a mile away; but the men were strung out in single file over a mile and it required some time to close up and form an attacking column. In the meantime it became plainly evident that the entire Yankee army was aroused, as we could distinctly hear the beating of the long roll in camp.

"And so it turned out that all the beautiful plans about

surprise and capture in a moment came to naught. However, as soon as Colonel Rust could get his men in shape we began moving upon the works, pushing our way through the woods to the edge of the clearing. Here Colonel Rust made a personal reconnaissance, exposing himself so recklessly as to get a bullet through his coat from a sentinel. He found the army fully on the alert and that the fort was completely surrounded by an almost impassable abatis, rendering it practically inaccessible. A council of the officers was held, and it was decided that there was nothing else to do but to get back home. I say home, for even the wretched camps on Greenbrier seemed like home to us.

". . . why was it the firing that occurred on our side was not heard by the troops on the other side awaiting the signal? I think this is easily explained. We were half a mile down the mountain side in a dense forest, which no doubt muffled the sound, and it must have been at least two or three miles on an air line intervening, and the sound did not carry that far. . . . I believe that but for being restrained by his officers he [Rust], would have hurled himself into that death trap on Cheat Mountain could he have found any reasonable number of men to follow him."[11]

In withdrawing his troops, Rust had seemingly forgotten about Company C, of the Thirty-first Virginia Infantry Regiment, which was deployed about a third of a mile west of the Cheat Mountain Fort. The Union skirmishers had worked strong flankers around both sides of the company and they were forced to withdraw about three-fourths of a mile to the rear, where they nervously awaited further orders.

Colonel Rust, remembering the neglected company, came back and discovered they did not have their knapsacks and other equipment which was removed as they had prepared earlier for the charge that never came. He angrily ordered them to go back and recover the missing paraphernalia. The company, in the extreme rear of the entire command, and in single file "about faced!" and warily started back on the unrelished mission.

Sergeant Bill Taylor and Private Henry Cammack were in the lead and when in sight of the discarded items they turned around to find only seven men of the entire company still behind. A few seconds later another quick glance revealed that the remaining seven had also disappeared, leaving only the two of them. By this time Union soldiers were punching bayonets into the baggage and shooting holes in it. Taylor insisted on opening fire, but Cammack persisted that discretion was the better part of valor and they retreated rapidly in order to catch up with the vanished company and the rear of the homeward bound column.[12]

On the Union side, the relief detail sent to Captain Coons under Captain Higgins had soon found the wagons whose horses and drivers had been captured earlier in the morning. As they hurried on, they met a cavalry soldier leading a wounded horse, and who stated that the enemy had collected in their rear at the junction of the pike and the path where Coons had turned off earlier and doubtlessly he and his party were cut off.

Back at Donelson's Confederate bivouac area on the ridge above Becky's Creek, the men had begun to stir before dawn and as soon as it was light enough to see they began to work on their guns and to draw out the loads, as not a single gun in the brigade would fire. Albert Tavel, a member of the Eighth Tennessee said: "Of all the picking, hammering, rattling of ram rods, rubbing, twisting out bullets and wet powder from old muskets ever witnessed, perhaps the occasion presented here was never surpassed. The wet loads had to be drawn from the guns and the guns thoroughly dried before they could be reloaded. To do this, much noise and confusion existed. The popping of caps, the shooting of blank cartridges, intermingled with the Babel-like confusion existing at the time, all contributed to the general 'hoodlum' on the mountain that morning. As soon as the guns were properly dried the Eighth reloaded their old smooth bore percussion cap muskets with dry powder and buck and ball cartridges."[13]

The Sixteenth Tennessee was armed with the older flintlock muskets and had to be even more careful to see their

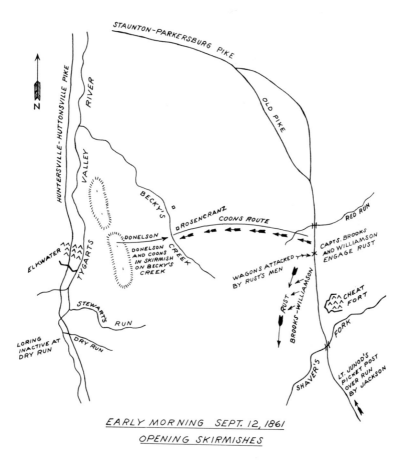

EARLY MORNING SEPT. 12, 1861
OPENING SKIRMISHES

guns were in firing condition, checking and examining the flints in addition to the unloading and drying procedure.[14]

Much of the Union force was armed with rifled muskets which had much greater range and better accuracy than the old Confederate smoothbores.

Union scouting parties had been sent out to scour the surrounding country and one of these detachments came very near to capturing General Lee on Becky's Creek. Lee had followed Donelson—who had exceeded his orders—to prevent his getting in trouble or being cut off. By the time Lee reached the old field on the evening of September 11 where Donelson turned up the mountain, it was so dark that he could not follow the trail, so he and his escort spent the night in the woods.[15] The next morning, Lee, accompanied by his aide and a few horsemen, was on his way to join General Donelson, and had scarcely emerged from a piece of woods when a Union cavalry detachment thundered along the road skirting the timber—too near to be comfortable—but galloping rapidly away on observing the proximity of Donelson's column of infantry.[16]

Lee and his aide continued to the top of the ridge where he contacted General Donelson and conferred for some time with him while looking over the immediate situation there, and awaiting the sound of Rust's attack. By 10:00 A.M. he realized something had gone wrong and ordered Donelson to withdraw the brigade into the valley.[17]

Over the ridge, near Elkwater, a battalion of the Second (West) Virginia under Colonel Moss, attracted by the racket of Donelson's Brigade, had formed in line of battle and the Confederates thought it was a Union column moving toward the ridge they occupied. At the same time, they could see other Union soldiers working their way up Becky's Creek, almost totally concealed in the dense underbrush, and believed a heavy advance was being made from that direction as well.

A detail was immediately dispatched from the Sixteenth Tennessee under Captain H. H. Dillard to move in advance of the main column pushing down the mountain. They were in a dense thicket with brush and tall weeds making it almost

Where Donelson turned up the mountain and Lee narrowly missed capture on Becky's Creek. Also scene of Captain Coons's fight with Donelson's men.

impossible to see anything in front of them while the remainder of the brigade moved behind in the narrow path that crossed the ridge.[18] As they moved toward the foot of the mountain, firing suddenly broke out, both sides later saying that the other opened fire first.

About this time the men of the Eighth Tennessee who were still on the ridge got their first look at General Lee as he had made his way toward them. One of the men said: "He looked like a hero. As he sat on his large white horse, half hid in the bushes, the greatness of the man could be easily distinguished, even by the casual observer, and alike by the common soldier. . . . Grand and dignified he sat there, the soldier and the Christian, a hero and a statesman, seeming to grasp the situation and to hold it in the hollow of his hand."[19]

The heavy advance that the Confederates imagined coming up Becky's Creek was Captain Coons's sixty men who had come over the path from Cheat Mountain to the Rosencranz house. They found the house deserted but the many tracks in the road showed there had been much activity in the vicinity recently.[20] Coons immediately sent out his scouts to reconnoiter, and in a short time they returned and reported that they had seen where cavalry had moved across the path and up the mountain toward Wagner's camp at Elkwater, which was just three miles distant.[21]

Private John R. McClure of Company G of the Fourteenth Indiana, who was one of the party, recalled that: "We looked across the valley up on the side of the mountain. We could see smoke and heard the snapping of caps as though they were cleaning their guns. Coons said, 'Boys, I expect those fellows are Colonel Wagner's pickets. We will have our breakfast over there.' "[22]

He then dispatched five scouts to follow the trail and investigate. They proceeded across a meadow about one hundred yards wide and up the mountain about fifty yards into the woods, and as firing broke out, Coons rushed his remaining men across the field at the "double-quick" to rescue his scouts, four of whom were wounded, two of whom were made prisoners.[23]

By this time, large numbers of the Sixteenth had joined

Colonel John Coons, then captain, Fourteenth Indiana Regiment. Photo from *Indiana at Antietam. Report of the Indiana Antietam Monument Commission,* 1911, opposite page 104.

Courtesy Indiana Historical Society Library

Captain Dillard's advance detail with the Eighth Tennessee furiously on the way to lend a hand. Captain Coons believed that his little detachment was receiving the fire of at least five hundred guns by now, and although they still couldn't see the Confederates, his little group fired five or six rounds at will into the woods and brush—both sides shooting high—and then retreated about fifty yards to the protection of a high bank of a creek.[24] Coons had already dispatched one of the cavalrymen to camp for reinforcements, but he was killed before reaching his destination.

The Southerners tried to form a line in the woods, but the underbrush and fire from Coons's little band was too much; though as more of their number joined them, they began to form in the field and Coons was again forced to retreat, this time behind some large fallen timber.[25]

Coons ordered his men to fire by platoons and this broke up a line formation or so, but as more men reached the foot of the mountain, the numbers became overpowering and the captain formed a skirmish line and fell into the timber back toward the Cheat Mountain camp. The movement was just in time as the Confederate battle line held this time and the little band barely escaped being flanked on both sides.

The captain's troubles were not over yet; because, when he had proceeded within a few miles of camp, it was discovered that the mountain was literally covered with the enemy, and he realized for the first time that Colonel Kimball had been attacked. He called his men together and informed them that in all probability there were three or four thousand Rebels between them and their camp; that for his part, he was resolved to die rather than become a prisoner, and called upon all those who were willing to cut their way through to camp. A unanimous assent was given and the men were deployed up the side of the mountain in skirmishing order.[26]

Back on Cheat Mountain the Coons relief detail under Captain Higgins proceeded cautiously; Lieutenant Green and men being deployed on the left of the road and Lieutenant Wood on the right. Captain Higgins held a group of men nearby—to the right and rear of the pike—to check the forward movement of any Confederates that might be deployed on the

road. After advancing a short way, the detail received a volley
from a strong hidden force of the enemy, but without loss.
The volley was returned and the advance continued. A second volley was received and returned. At this point Lieutenant Green located the Confederates, concealed at the right
of the road, and poured in a destructive fire on them until
they fled across the pike.

At the same time, Captain Higgins saw a large body of men
retreating in confusion, and in so doing, falling back upon
what appeared to be a larger force drawn in line of battle.
Actually Captain Coons's skirmish line had fallen upon the
rear of the Confederates now in retreat from Higgins's fire
and scattered them in confusion; the surprised Rebels believed that they had fallen into an ambush and presented the
scene Higgins now surveyed. Coons's men poured three quick
volleys into the Rebels who looked like doctors, Negroes,
quartermasters, and what not, and they broke and ran; but
Confederates were everywhere and Coons could not go forward. He gave the order to "right face!" and the little detail
moved out—Indian fashion—through the woods as quickly as
possible.[27]

Captain Higgins redeployed his line, but ordered them to
make no advance, determining to hold the position until the
arrival of reinforcements. After waiting half an hour, Major
Harrow of the Fourteenth Indiana came up with two companies and immediately sent forward a squad to reconnoiter.
They soon returned, bringing in two prisoners who said the
force was General Anderson's brigade of Tennesseans. The
squad had fallen upon the left wing of Anderson's line, and
when learning their strength, Major Harrow ordered Higgins
to draw in his men and post them as an advanced guard two
miles nearer the camp. The order was complied with and the
position was held without further action until the detail was
relieved the next morning. The Union had two men wounded
in the skirmish and the Confederate losses were never officially reported.[28]

While Captain Higgins was early engaged with the enemy,
Colonel Kimball was informed that the Confederates were
moving in his front above the hill east of the fort, where a

picket station was commanded that day by Lieutenant August Junod, Company E, Fourteenth Indiana. The Confederates soon surrounded the picket, consisting of thirty-five
men, and in the ensuing skirmish, Junod and one private were
killed, while another escaped by pretending he was dead and
falling to the ground. The remainder of the picket force made
a hurried and rather disorderly withdrawal to the fort.

The Confederate force that had moved on this position
was an advance guard of General H. R. Jackson's column
ordered ahead by Colonel Edward Johnson. Very early in the
morning Johnson had taken five men from each company of
the First and Twelfth Georgia regiments and formed the
guard of one hundred men whom he placed under command
of Lieutenant Dawson of the Twelfth and ordered him to
make contact with the Union pickets by another road.

Johnson, himself, then took a company of the Twelfth
Georgia and made an advance guard of it to follow the
Staunton-Parkersburg Pike, with the First Georgia fifty yards
behind. The Twelfth followed, with the artillery behind it,
and Colonel W. C. Scott's Forty-fourth Virginia Infantry
Regiment brought up the rear, which regiment the feisty
Confederate, James Hall, justly or unjustly referred to as the
grandest cowards in the army.[29]

Colonel Johnson took five men and moved out in front of
the advance guard in the heavy fog to probe the road for an
ambush and to locate the Federal pickets. The march continued for about a mile in this manner when suddenly there
was a sharp report of a rifle and a bullet whistled by Colonel
Johnson's head as the picket post was located the hard way.
The colonel and his five men immediately fell back to the
advance guard in a turn on the road and Johnson, not knowing the strength of the concealed force, sent scouts up the
side of the mountain, which was on his left, to prevent a
flanking attempt. They remained in this position for about
half an hour and the Union pickets thinking the Confederates
had withdrawn, moved into the open and Confederate fire
wounded one and drove the remainder into a hasty retreat.
The Confederate column now started to advance slowly with

General Edward Johnson
Then colonel, Twelfth Georgia Infantry Regiment.
Courtesy National Archives

Shaver's Fork of Cheat River below the Cheat Summit Fort.

General Jackson and Colonels Johnson and Ramsey in the lead.[30]

In the meantime, Lieutenant Dawson's party, guided by a local resident, had gotten close enough to the Cheat Fort—in position earlier than Rust's column—to hear the drums beat for guard mount and the bands play "Annie Laurie," "Jordan Is a Hard Road to Travel," and other selections. As they lay under cover, one of their number accidently discharged his rifle and this brought a Union soldier from the picket down the road to investigate; the Confederates fired and he fell dead in the road. Attracted by the firing, about twenty-five of the Federals came hurriedly down the road, saw their dead comrade and fired a volley into the woods. Lieutenant Dawson gave the order to "charge!" and as the Rebels drove for the road, the picket force scattered into the woods, but not before another Federal was killed from their fire.[31]

This was Lieutenant Junod's picket post, above the hill east of the fort, that Lieutenant Dawson had attacked and dispersed.

After the firing ceased, Dawson, feeling that it was unsafe to remain so near the Federal camp with so small a force, reformed the guard and they began their march down the mountain. They were expecting to encounter the reserve Union picket, but in a sharp turn in the road, were confronted by a column of troops marching in fours and only a hundred yards away. One of the guard sang out, "Here they are boys!" and the firing broke out immediately.

Three men were shot down and Dawson seeing that they were outnumbered, ordered them to fall below the road, which was done without the least urging. The fire slackened for a moment and then came the order: "Charge 'em!" Up into the road they went and discovered they were fighting their own men—the main column that had followed the pike—"cease firing! we are Georgians! Hurrah for Jeff Davis!" rang out from almost a hundred throats.

Ed Johnson, in command of the Twelfth Georgia, was riding towards the head of the column and hearing the cry, yelled: "They are liars boys. Pop it to 'em! Pop it to 'em!" The mistake was soon discovered, however, and the firing ceased. Three men had been killed and a number wounded by the mutual and unfortunate error. One of the victims, a man named Felder, had told his messmates before leaving camp that he would be killed—one of those strange premonitions that unfortunately proved all too true—another was shot through the thigh, the ball cutting an artery, causing him to bleed to death. His comrades related that blood gushed down the road for a distance of fifteen feet—in the absence of proper medical care. The third was shot in the heart and killed instantly. After the wounded had been cared for, the guard was reformed in front of the brigade and they marched back to a position in front of the Federal camp to await Colonel Rust to open the attack on the rear.

As General Anderson's column had prepared to face what the morning of the twelfth would bring forth, Dr. Charles Quintard, the chaplain with the First Tennessee Infantry Regiment, remembered that: "In the morning I was well soaked, my finger ends were corrugated and my whole body chilled through. I was hungry also, but all I could get to eat was one tough biscuit that almost defied my most vigorous assaults. We were ordered to be on the Parkersburg Pike that day [Thursday], at daybreak. To show how little we understood of the art of war at that time, soon after we started, a well mounted horseman passed half-way down the line of the regiment without detection. He proved to be a Federal courier. Lieutenant Colonel Sevier finally halted him and said in surprise; 'Why you're a Yankee!' To which the courier coolly replied; 'I'm so thankful you found me out; I was so afraid of being shot.' . . . Half a mile further on brought us to the Parkersburg Pike, three and a half miles from Cheat Mountain Pass [Summit].[32] The First Tennessee was at the head of a column towards Cheat Pass [Summit].[33] In about ten minutes a body of the enemy, about one hundred strong, in ambush on the opposite side of the road and only about twenty-five yards from our troops, began firing into our left, composed of the companies from Pulaski, Columbia and Murfreesboro. The enemy were completely concealed but our men stood the fire nobly. Not a man flinched. After two or three volleys had been fired, Captain Field ordered a charge and the enemy fled."[34]

This was undoubtedly Captain Higgins's detail that the First Tennessee met. Both sides thought the other was in ambush, but actually the thick brush and undergrowth probably hid them from each other's view. The details vary somewhat as to which side advanced and which withdrew but the eventual outcome remained unaffected by these claims.

Dr. J. R. Buist, a physician with the brigade, wrote: "At last on the third day, we reached our position, having come so quietly that the enemy were completely surprised. Our business was to prevent reinforcements going from one point to another, while the attack was to be made at three other points. Soon after reaching the road we had a heavy skirmish with the pickets and scouts, in which we lost two killed, two missing, and seventeen wounded, some mortally. After this the enemy retired. We anxiously waited to hear the report of cannon from the general attack, which was to be made that morning."[35]

Shortly after Colonel Kimball learned that the Confederates had moved in on Lieutenant Junod's picket post, he was informed that Captains Brook's and Williamson's men were driving the enemy engaged in their area to the Union right flank. Kimball immediately dispatched two companies, one from the Fourteenth Indiana, Company A, under Captain Foote and one company from the Twenty-fourth Ohio to move up Shaver's Fork of Cheat River and cut off the enemy's retreat, this being part of Rust's column. The two companies with Captain Foote and the captain of the Ohio company moved about two miles up the river and Lieutenant Robert Catterson, with a small detachment, was sent up still farther, and he in turn sent two men in advance, who saw the Rebels coming up with two of the twenty-five men who had been taken prisoners. The two men in advance each selected a man and pulled trigger; one Confederate fell dead, but the second man's gun failed to discharge and they took two prisoners and recaptured two Ohio boys.[36] Colonel Kimball added that the Rebels were scattered and several killed.[37]

When Captain Coons had decided to break off further

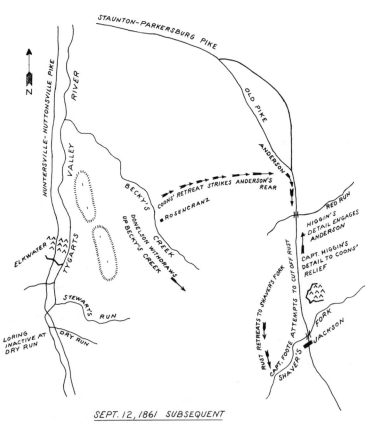

SEPT. 12, 1861 SUBSEQUENT
SKIRMISHES AND ACTION

contact with Anderson's Confederate brigade he marched his men, single file through the woods, the same being littered with baggage, blankets, knapsacks, coats, haversacks, and various other assorted items. They finally sat down to rest and had to admit to themselves that they were lost and felt surrounded on all sides by the enemy. Even the redoubtable Coons didn't know what to do and finally one of Bracken's Cavalry, a bright-eyed boy of eighteen years, said he could lead them out and did, arriving in camp on the west side about sunset.[38]

Coons came into camp with less than half a pair of trousers covering him, and that portion in tatters, but in a few minutes after his arrival had on a whole pair of breeches that bore a striking resemblance to those usually worn by Colonel Kimball. All the party was cut, scratched, and bruised by the torturous trip, clothes were in rags, and many had no shoes. Few at the fort had ever expected to see them again so their arrival touched off a wild scene of great joy among their comrades and friends.

Colonel Kimball claimed killing over a hundred during the day, wounding a greater number, and taking a total of thirteen prisoners; but the Confederates never confirmed these losses and they were in all probability over estimated, a practice common in all wars. The Confederate force never at any time got close enough to the Cheat Fort to give Captain Philip Daum's (W.) Virginia Battery an opportunity to fire on them.

Down in Cheat Mountain Pass, three companies of the Thirteenth Indiana under Captain Clinton had spent the day on the pike in order to hold that point, while the remainder of the regiment was deployed at the head of the pass to watch the movements of Anderson and to hastily construct fieldworks.

General Reynolds's headquarters were at the pass—along with the Thirteenth Indiana, under Colonel Sullivan, two pieces of artillery, and Reynolds's cavalry escort—but he personally directed the movements at Elkwater, temporarily moving his headquarters there, putting unnumbered hours in the saddle and sleeping little, maintaining a constant state of alert.[39]

He had the stores at the Pass removed to Huttonsville, putting the Tygart's Valley River between them and the danger of a raid.

The only action the Thirteenth Indiana saw on the twelfth was a picket post encounter in the direction of Elkwater and a brief skirmish a scouting party of that regiment had with the Confederates.[40]

Chapter Twelve
Silent Defeat

All the Confederates had waited most anxiously for the firing of Rust's guns as the signal to open the general engagement. A. L. Long said: "It was anxiously expected from early dawn throughout the day. On every side was continuously heard, 'What has become of Rust?' The Tennesseeans under Anderson became so impatient that they requested to be led to the attack without waiting for Rust, but Anderson thought that he must be governed by the letter of his instructions and declined granting the request of his men."[1]

Captain Walter H. Taylor wrote: "General Jackson worried the enemy considerably by attacking his advanced guard on the first top of the mountain, only awaiting the signal from Rust to press forward earnestly with his entire command. Hours passed and no signal was heard! What could have happened? Enough time had lapsed to enable the troops to reach Centretop, unless prevented by some unexpected impediment.

"Would Rust *never* attack? Alas! he never did!"[2]

It will be remembered that Lee had personally withdrawn Donelson's Brigade about 10:00 A.M. and sent them up Becky's Creek and ultimately over the long route back to camp. He had eventually got a courier over to General Anderson, ordering his return, and they had retired about four o'clock in the afternoon.[3]

General Jackson had remained across Cheat River in front of the Cheat Fort all day, also awaiting the missing signal until late in the afternoon and then retired.[4]

During the course of the day, the many small Union details and companies marching along narrow paths, through the massive timber—with the Confederates just getting a glimpse of them in the thick brush or in the high weeds of an occasional open field—gave the impression of regiments on the move where only companies were involved.

Confederate prisoners afterwards related how, as they lay in their hiding places, the conviction crept over them that

Colonel Walter H. Taylor
Then captain. Lee's aide-de-camp.
Courtesy Library of Congress

instead of surrounding the Union forces that they themselves were securely encircled.[5] Distant views of troops marching along both pike and path added to their conviction, and thus, the hounds mentally found themselves occupying the role of the fox.

The Federal units not realizing the numbers that opposed them, boldly reconnoitered and attacked upon numerous occasions when the enemy appeared in front of them. To say they showed forth a bold front would be a gross understatement as with each flurry of fighting they gained confidence by leaps and bounds and one Indiana soldier said they felt like they could whip the whole Rebel Army. As usual the old adage that "nothing succeeds like success" was working full time that day.

Colonel Kimball, in his report of September 14, concluded: "I think my men have done wonders, and ask God to bless them. The woods are literally covered with the baggage, coats, and haversacks of the enemy. Though almost naked, my command is ready to move forward."[6]

Kimball's troops were literally near to being naked as the clothing drawn at the state camps had been of poor quality and had soon begun to show signs of decay, with the wearers being soaking wet two-thirds of the time. The government shoes were of little protection against wet feet and the jackets and trousers were soon only tattered rags—all the products of profit greedy manufacturers taking advantage of the state and national governments. Many bitter letters were written by these soldiers to those back home complaining about the quality of the clothing. After a scout through the thickets and among the rocks, climbing mountains, and descending ravines, it was not uncommon to see a detail return with little more than waistbands left of what had once been a poor pair of trousers.[7]

General Reynolds stated in his report of the action: "So rested matters at dark on the 12th, with heavy forces in front and in plain sight of both posts, communications cut off, and the supply train for the mountains loaded with provisions that were needed."[8]

Neither General Lee nor General Loring had heard from

Colonel Rust on the twelfth and the first official word from
him is a letter written to General Loring from Camp Bartow
at 10:00 P.M. on the thirteenth. Rust had returned to quarters at Camp Bartow in obedience to undated instructions
from General H. R. Jackson.

From the contents of Jackson's note, it appears that it was
written on the morning of the thirteenth, the note reading
thus:

> Dear Colonel: Return to camp with your command. So soon
> as you arrive, address a letter to General Loring, explaining the
> failure and the reasons for it. Show this to Captain Neil, quarter-
> master, and let him at once furnish an express ready to take your
> letter by the near route. If possible, get the postmaster, Mr. Arbo-
> gast, to go, and go rapidly and at once. Say in your letter that I
> am in possession of the first summit of Cheat Mountain, and in
> hopes of something going on in Tygart's Valley, and shall retain
> command of it until I receive orders from headquarters. It may
> bring on an engagement, but I am prepared, and shall whip them
> if they come. Very truly yours,
>   H. R. JACKSON
> P.S.—I cannot write here. Enclose this scrawl in your own letter.
> You had better return yourself at once to camp, leaving your
> command to follow. We had several skirmishes yesterday and
> killed several of the enemy.

It seems that General Jackson had learned of Colonel
Rust's failure before he had written the note ordering him
and his command back to camp. Rust complied with the
order immediately but his brigade was several days straggling
into camp through the rugged mountain country.

Rust's written report to General Loring was as follows:

> Camp Bartow, Sept. 13, 1861—10: p.m.
> General: The expedition against Cheat Mountain failed. My com-
> mand consisted of between 1500 and 1600 men. Got there at the
> appointed time, notwithstanding the rain. Seized a number of
> their pickets and scouts. Learned from them that the enemy was
> between 4,000 and 5,000 strong, and they reported them to be
> strongly fortified. Upon a reconnaissance their representations
> were fully corroborated. A fort or block house on the point or
> elbow of the road, intrenchments on the south and outside the
> intrenchments and all around up to the road heavy and impassible
> abatis, if the enemy were not behind them, Colonel Barton, my
> Lieutenant Colonel, and all the field officers declared it would be

madness to make an attack. We learned from the prisoners they were aware of your movements, and had been telegraphed for re-enforcements, and I heard three pieces of artillery pass down toward your encampment while we were seeking to make an assault on them.

I took the assistant commissary, and for one regiment I found upon his person a requisition for 930 rations; also a letter indicating they had very little subsistence. I brought only one prisoner back with me. The cowardice of the guard (not Arkansian) permitted the others to escape. Spies had evidently communicated our movements to the enemy. The fort was completed as reported by the different prisoners examined separately, and another in the process of construction. We got near enough to see the enemy in the trenches beyond the abatis. The most of my command behaved admirably. Some I would prefer to be without on any expedition.

General Jackson requests me to say to you that he is in possession of the first summit of Cheat Mountain, and hopes you are doing something in the Tygart's Valley, and will retain command of it until he receives orders from your quarters. My own opinion is that there is nothing to be gained by occupying that mountain. It will take a heavy force to take the Pass [Summit], and at a heavy loss. I knew the enemy had four times my force; but for the abatis we would have made the assault. We could not get them to make it. The general says, in his note to me, his occupying Cheat Mountain may bring on an engagement, but he is prepared and will whip them if they come. I see from the postscript that he requests his note to be enclosed to you. I can only say that all human power could do towards success in my expedition failed of success. The taking of the picket looked like a providential interposition. I took the first one myself, being at the head of the column when I got to the road.

In great haste, very respectfully your obedient servant,

A. RUST
Colonel &c.
General LORING, Commanding &c.[9]

The one great opportunity since Loring had lingered at Huntersville had come and gone. With all units in the right position at dawn or early morning of September 12, the moment for the success of the campaign had arrived, but it didn't last long nor did it return.

Many things have been said about the conduct of the campaign. True, Loring tarried much too long with the initial preparations, and much bad weather and sickness prevailed. Some say the terrain beat Lee—that he didn't have room to maneuver. Lee, himself, in a letter to Governor Letcher said: "but for the rainstorm I have no doubt that it would have succeeded." Others lay the blame to the fact that some of the Confederate soldiers after a very wet night, fired their arms in an effort to clear them, thus losing the element of surprise, but the troops that fired were Donelson's men, mostly snapping caps and firing a few blanks on the mountain between Becky's Creek and the Tygart's Valley and certainly didn't alarm or arouse anyone in the Cheat Summit Fort, four or five miles away—the first alarm at that point being the capture of the teamsters driving the daily wagon train.

The fact alone remains, however, that at dawn, regardless of slow preparations, sickness, bad weather, difficult terrain, or any other reason, all the troops were in place just like the Confederate commanders wanted them. Regardless of what had happened, all difficulties had been overcome, the plan was on schedule and just as planned. It seems only logical that reasons given for failure prior to dawn September 12 could not be a major factor in the Confederate defeat.

One element that is unmeasurable after more than a hundred years is what part the events leading up to the morning of September 12, 1861, had on the mental attitude and the physical attributes of the Confederates as a fighting force.

Most Southern authorities agree that the plans were excellent and that their fulfillment was letter perfect up to that point. The question is, what happened? The plan was ready for execution, but Colonel Rust *took some prisoners who told him that inside the Cheat Mountain Bastion were some four thousand to five thousand Federal troops with heavy reinforcements on the way.* The Confederates looked, they saw, they believed. The will to attack was gone. The elements of surprise, position, and plan were now lost.

The Confederates saw just what the prisoners told them, although it wasn't quite that way. Colonel Rust said their story was fully corroborated, and the three thousand men that garrisoned the mountain fortress and its approaches that day possibly looked to be four or five thousand as Rust reported. The colonel and the men that were with him there were to perform admirably and fearlessly on innumerable

Present remains of Old Cheat Fort.

occasions later in the war and to prove themselves many times. Under greater difficulties would positions be taken and victories won.

Some of the very real heroes and prime instruments of the victory of September 12, 1861, on Cheat Mountain were the prisoners who concocted the story about two thousand non-existent Federal infantry in the fort and equally fictitious heavy reinforcements supposedly on the way. The story was firmly planted in Rust's mind, took root, and grew until he hesitated, wavered, and the battle was silently lost without even starting.

Much credit is due the three hundred Indiana and Ohio volunteers who fought so aggressively and who were so determined not to be defeated. Stationed in a fine defensive position, they didn't hesitate to come out and carry the fight to the Confederates in a fine offensive display of courage and daring.

As the day of September 12, 1861, had drawn to a close, opportunity for success in the campaign was gone and Lee was defeated; Rust had never fired and the various attacks were never launched.

Captain Walter Taylor summed it up by saying: "Detached, discovered, without knowledge of the cause of Rust's silence, the other commands were powerless for good, and occupied with the necessity of providing for their own safety, it only remained to have them recalled to their former positions. On the next day Colonel Rust personally reported to General Lee. The only cause given for his no action was the same as heretofore.

"Some thought it a proper matter for a court of inquiry or for trial by court martial, but neither was ever had. . . ."[10]

Chapter Thirteen
Standoff in the Valley

While all the events described were transpiring on Cheat Mountain, Loring's column had appeared within sight of the Federal outpost on the Elkwater front, located approximately a mile and a half in front of the main entrenchments.

From the outpost's view, the Confederates seemed to be resting on their arms, waiting apparently for an order to attack. They sent out skirmishers to their front and on the flanks, keeping up a lively fire with the restless Union pickets, but no action came from the long columns, with artillery strung along the road and the infantry resting in the meadow below.[1]

Major J. Warren Keifer of the Third Ohio Infantry Regiment—later Speaker of the House of Representatives—had been sent with a detachment of four companies of his regiment as grand guard to assume picket and scouting duties. His outpost was on a mountain spur just northwest of the mouth of Elkwater Fork on the west side of the Huntersville-Huttonsville Pike.

This position covered the Elkwater Road from Brady's Gate, the pike, the narrow valley of the Tygart's and afforded a fine point of observation up the valley towards the Confederates. Here, Reynolds determined to first stubbornly resist the advance of the enemy and ordered temporary works constructed; consequently Keifer had, at times, artillery and various other detachments assigned to him. Reynolds also located another detachment on the east side of the river with similar instructions.[2]

Back at the fortifications, the Federal soldiers stood on top of their entrenchments peering up the winding valley, trying to get an occasional glimpse of the enemy, while at the higher elevations of the lookout and outpost stations the whole panorama was plainly visible.

As the game of waiting continued, mounted Federal officers, orderlies, and squads of dragoons—anxious to attract the attention of the vast audience—would dash up to a house or a

Looking from Elkwater to Loring's position on Dry Run.

clump of bushes and occasionally draw a sharp rattle of musket fire which would result in a rapid withdrawal, quickly followed by a squad of Rebel sharpshooters in pursuit. Union riflemen would immediately double-quick to their comrade's rescue and at times during the exchanges a horse would flounder in the mire, compelling the rider to execute a spontaneous acrobatic maneuver that brought laughter from all in sight.[3]

Along toward evening, as the setting sun cast the shadows of the hills across the valley, General J. J. Reynolds, accompanied by the colonels of several regiments and his escort, rode out among the Union skirmishers. As he swept the enemy position with his glass, the Rebel gunners sent a twelve-pound shot down the valley that fell short. Reynolds hastily wrote a note and handed it to an orderly and in a few moments one of Loomis's ten-pound Parrot guns was out and hurling shell at the head of the enemy column. The Confederates quickly withdrew out of range and partially out of view and Loomis turned his gun on the houses and bushes which concealed the reserves of their flanking skirmishers and soon scattered them, ending the action for the day of September 12, although in the night, Loring, during a rain and under cover of darkness, sent a small body of troops to the rear of Major Keifer's grand-guard position and actually gained a point on the spur of the mountain behind and above him, but the attack though a surprise, was feebly executed and a brisk, spirited return fire and countercharge scattered the attacking force.[4]

General Reynolds, determined to open communications between Elkwater and Cheat Mountain, ordered the Thirteenth Indiana under Colonel Sullivan to make contact by the Staunton-Parkersburg Turnpike with the Cheat Mountain garrison. The Thirteenth was stationed at Cheat Mountain Pass which was nine miles west of the fort and at the foot of Cheat Mountain. He also ordered the greater part of the Third Ohio and Second (West) Virginia under Colonels Marrow and Moss, respectively, to the same objective, except they were to move by the path from Elkwater to the top of the mountain. Both commands moved out at 3:00 A.M. on

Loring's position at Dry Run looking toward Elkwater.

September 13 to fall on the enemy simultaneously, if possible. With the little information available, General Reynolds had perceptively sensed that there would be no attack made at Elkwater the next day and that Colonel Kimball would still be holding the Cheat Summit Fort.

The two relief columns marched to the summit, reopened communications and secured the provision train, finding the defenders very much in command of the situation.

General Reynolds reported that before the relief columns reached the summit on September 13 that the defenders of the fort fought another action and again routed the Confederates, and on the fourteenth and fifteenth, fought similar actions.[5]

General H. R. Jackson's men were the only Confederates left on the mountain and Lavender Ray, who was a member of the First Georgia Infantry Regiment of that command and who wrote a detailed letter of the affair, mentions no action after September 12, but states they were in place before the fort each day, finally withdrawing on Monday, September 16, 1861. His account in his own words follows: "We then advanced in sight of the enemy's camp [September 12] and formed in an old field where we remained until four o'clock p.m. waiting for Lee to attack them in the rear which he did not do and we were ordered back to camp.[6] We then began to march to camp being almost broken down with fatigue. We marched until we came within a few miles of camp when General Jackson received a dispatch and we were immediately astonished by the order, 'Counter march by left file!' It was almost like a death knell to me. I was broken down with fatigue, my feet ached and my shoulders and hips were sore from carrying a heavy cartridge box and haversack packed with food for two days, and a large shawl and canteen full of water. The idea of going back miles to fight seemed like death, but I hurried up determined to go as long as I could. But we only went about a mile when we camped in an old field. We made a large fire and I warmed some coffee I had in my canteen (having brought it as it was good to quench thirst when cold) and ate a cracker then wrapped my shawl around me and threw myself upon the grass to catch a few hours sleep in the open air with my accoutrements around me and my gun by my side, not knowing at what moment I should be aroused. I had a troubled sleep that night which was Thursday, for often I would get so cold that I would have to get up and warm at the fire and I could not help thinking, for a few minutes of the soft warm feather beds at home. I had been all day with our company at the head of the army. . . .

"We aroused at dawn of day [September 13] and was ordered to fall in.[7] General Jackson then told the army if any soldier went back to camp on the plea of sickness and when examined was not sick his life should not be spared by his mercy. Some of the men had gone home the day before on that plea, who were perfectly well. . . . We then marched toward the enemy and General Jackson made our regiment a speech on the way. He complemented us highly and as he passed looked every man in the eye. Someone wanted him to put the 12th [Georgia] in front to take the battery but he had more confidence in the 1st Georgia and always gave us the post of honor.[8] When we arrived near the enemy he put our regiment in ambush and tried to draw the enemy out but could not do so. In the evening the army (except a hundred) retired to the camping place of the night before. The hundred was a guard composed of six men from each company. . . . The guard was divided into squads of six men each and stationed up and down the road to watch the enemy. Our provisions were now near out and I ate that night, one or two crackers and a piece of fat meat. . . . We remained that night watching every moment for them, expecting every moment for the enemy to rush upon us then it would be fire your gun and get away who can; but nothing of interest happened that night. In the morning [September 14] Lieutenant Dawson who is a very brave man with little judgement carried our guard half a mile closer to the enemy and farther than anyone had gone when the enemy was near.[9] We expected every moment the enemy to fire upon us from ambush or rush in overwhelming numbers upon our little band but we marched on and found blankets and guns which the enemy's pickets had thrown away when they heard us coming. We then went back to the old field and were welcomed by our company who said they never expected to see us again. After getting something to eat we slept awhile, then built us an arbor to sleep under. The next day was Sunday [September 15] we did not do anything but relieve our pickets. Monday our army again advanced and prepared to fortify a hill in sight of the enemy. I had begun to work . . . and we were ordered back to camp."[10]

Walter Clark, who was an orderly sergeant in the First Georgia, in writing of his experience on Cheat Mountain said: "As the attack on the rear had for some reason failed to materialize, General Jackson after remaining on the mountain four days, returned to his old camp."[11] This statement is in full agreement with Ray's and it would seem that there was no further action after the twelfth.

J. T. Pool also said there was no other attempt to attack the fort after September 12.[12]

Possibly, Reynolds had, in the excitement, received some unreliable reports from some unnamed source and incorporated them in his report, which as a whole is rather vague and incomplete, along with what would appear to be some inaccuracies.

After Donelson's skirmish with Coons's detail on the twelfth, Lee had ordered the brigade withdrawn and they had made their way up Becky's Creek on the first leg of the weary march back to camp. Lee accompanied them most of the day and word had passed through the brigade how he had spent hours in the saddle in order to contact them and give their dangerous situation his personal attention. He made his way up and down the column, sometimes in the front, sometimes in the rear, and on the top of a high mountain—when the exhausted men were allowed to fall out for a much needed rest—he rode near the center of the brigade with the men scattered in utter fatigue. Suddenly, someone raised a cheer and soon the whole brigade had taken it up and for a few moments the tops of the mountains resounded and reverberated with the wild shouts of the men in honor of the general. As the echos rang out on the mountain wilderness, Lee lifted his hat and bowing to the men on the right and on the left rode off—never to be seen by many of them again.

After resting awhile, the hungry men set out on impromptu foraging parties and in a few minutes a herd of fine cattle was discovered nearby—browsing on the mountaintop—a musket shot rang out and others soon followed until the whole herd lay slaughtered. Little camp fires sprang up, and as soon as a hide could be stripped off, a piece of meat was cut, and without salt or bread was hung in the blaze—on stick or ramrod—and cooked or scorched, no men ever ate sweeter meat. They declared that no king or potentate ever relished his most sumptuous banquet more, and the place was forever remembered by the two regiments as "Beef Mountain."

Almost half of the men were barefooted from the hard march; with feet raw and bleeding, they took pieces of the raw hides and bound them around their feet as best they could. The night was spent on the mountain and on the following morning the painful march continued back toward their former camps.[13]

On the afternoon of September 13, over in the Tygart's Valley, Major W. H. F. Lee, Confederate commander of cavalry, was ordered to make a reconnaissance in front of Elkwater to determine the Federal position and locate avenues of approach.

Major Lee, with a mounted detachment, was accompanied by Lieutenant Colonel John Augustine Washington of General Lee's staff. They had scouted the country in front of the Union lines and were in the vicinity of Elkwater Fork of the Tygart's Valley River near the Elk Road when Major Lee, conscious of the nearness of the Federal pickets, decided their mission was accomplished and proposed to return, but Colonel Washington, in a spirit of daring and eagerness, urged that they venture farther.

At this time, Company K, Captain Kloenne, of the Seventeenth Indiana Infantry was on picket, posted about a mile in front of the Elkwater Camp. In the exercise of extraordinary vigilance, as exerted for several days past under Reynold's orders, Colonel Hascall had sent Company E, of the Seventeenth under Captain Stough, to reconnoiter beyond the picket post occupied by Kloenne. This company had pro-

ceeded a half mile or farther beyond the picket when they
came to a long narrow pass or defile in which ran Elkwater
Fork, flanked on the right by a mountainside covered with
dense undergrowth—a prime spot for an ambush by hidden
troops. Captain Stough, in precaution, detailed ten men
under Sergeant J. J. Weiler as flankers to scour the hillside in
advance of the company.

The sergeant, with two men, Corporal William L. Birney
and Private William L. Johnson, proceeded together in a line
parallel to the road, the other eight men being farther up the
hillside and keeping abreast of the three, while the remainder
of the company halted in position, concealed by a curve in
the road.

Just at this juncture of affairs on the Federal side, Colonel
Washington had succeeded in persuading Major Lee to further
risk. The main body of their cavalry was ordered to remain in
position on a hilltop and taking two men along, Lee and
Washington proceeded to a point where they could see down
the ravine—perhaps a half mile—at the distant end of what
appeared to be a vidette, that is, a mounted sentinel. Colonel
Washington exclaimed, "Let us capture that fellow on a gray
horse." Overpersuaded, Major Lee agreed. Directing the two
cavalrymen to remain where they were, he and Colonel Washington charged down the ravine, "Believing" Lee said, "that
the vidette would probably empty his carbine and retreat."
When about half the distance was covered they came directly
opposite Sergeant Weiler and party, who had just reached a
mound of earth, where they had halted, alerted by the sound
of the approaching horsemen.

As the riders came opposite the concealed Federals, they
right wheeled across the road to pass part of a fallen tree,
presenting their backs to the flankers who recognized them as
the enemy by a white patch on Colonel Washington's cap.
They raised their guns, carefully aimed, and fired almost simultaneously, the three balls passing through Colonel Washington, whose horse, a fine bay charger, suddenly wheeled as
his rider fell, and ran back, following Major Lee who retreated hastily—as the three balls that felled Washington
passed through his body and struck Major Lee's horse wound-

Site of Lieutenant Colonel Washington's death on Elkwater Fork.

ing it and causing it to fall. Lee continued his retreat, running for some distance up the bed of the creek, as protection from further fire and as Washington's horse neared he quickly mounted and made good his escape.

The flankers immediately ran to Colonel Washington who, trying to rise on his elbow, was in a gasping, dying condition. The three bullets struck near to each other in his back, passing out his chest—one through a letter in his blouse pocket, the second just below the pocket, while the third one cut the top of his pistol belt.

The entire company was soon upon the spot and Colonel Washington asked for a drink, which was given to him and he died, saying no more. A litter was formed from guns and accoutrements upon which the body was carried back to the picket post, where an ambulance was brought to carry him into camp. His identity was unknown until Colonel Hascall met them and observed the name of John A. Washington upon the cuffs of his gauntlets and a napkin in his haversack. On reaching camp, Captain Loomis of the Michigan Battery was sent for—being a previous acquaintance—and his identity was established.

It was very early in the war and the name, Washington of Mount Vernon, the great-grandnephew of the first president, invoked an unusual amount of interest and excitement and the incidents as well as the correspondence that followed were seemingly unprecedented and unusual, partly macabre, partly highly respectful and tender.

Captain John Levering made an examination of the person of Colonel Washington. He had a pair of heavy pistols and a large knife attached to a belt around his body, a small powder flask, a field glass, a pair of spurs, buck gauntlets, an old-fashioned gold watch and fob chain, letters, and a map of the country on the Union front, along with some coins. His sword, which was tied to the pommel of his saddle, was with his horse. The body was carefully disposed and placed in the camp hospital (farm dwelling) until morning, when it was returned to his friends.

Early on the following morning (September 14, 1861) as directed by General Reynolds, Colonel Hascall took charge of

an escort conveying the body in an ambulance driven by
Sergeant Weiler, and carrying communication from General
Reynolds to the Confederate commander, as follows:

Headquarters,
Sept. 14, 1861.

TO COMMANDING OFFICER,
    Confederate Forces, Tygart's Valley
    Sir:—By direction of the General commanding this post I for-
ward, under flag of truce, the remains of Colonel John A. Washington, that his friends may with more certainty obtain them.
There was not time last night after his recognition to communicate.

Very respectfully,
Geo. S. Rose,
A. A. General.

Proceeding beyond the lines with a flag of truce displayed,
they reached the outer picket post, which was on that day
under the command of Major J. Warren Kiefer of the Third
Ohio Volunteers, and a flag of truce from General Lee in the
charge of Colonel W. E. Starke was met, bearing a note of
inquiry as follows:

HEADQUARTERS CAMP ON VALLEY RIVER
Sept. 14, 1861.

TO THE GENERAL COMMANDING U. S. TROOPS:
    HUTTONSVILLE, VA.
    General:—Lieutenant-Colonel John A. Washington, my Aide-
de-Camp, whilst riding yesterday with a small escort was fired
upon by your pickets and I fear killed. Should such be the case, I
request that you will deliver to me his body, or should he be a
prisoner in your hands, that I be informed of his condition.
    I have the honor to be your obedient servant,

R. E. LEE,
General Commanding.

Information of the death of Colonel Washington having
been sent to the Confederate Commander, an ambulance
with mounted escort, under command of Major W. H. F. Lee,
came to receive the body. The transfer was made, and the
detachments returned to their respective camps. In the disposal of the confiscated articles taken from the person of
Colonel Washington the following correspondence occurred:

WAR DEPARTMENT
Oct. 22, 1861.

BRIGADIER GENERAL J. J. REYNOLDS.
CAMP ELK WATER, VA.

Sir:—Through the hands of Captain H. Jones Brooks I have the honor to acknowledge the receipt of an army revolver found on the person of Colonel John A. Washington. I shall always prize it as a memorable relic of the present glorious struggle for freedom and the Union.

To the brave Sergeant Leiber (?), of the Seventeenth Indiana Regiment, who enjoys the honor of having made this notorious rebel leader bite the dust, you will, in the name of the War Department, present the other revolver and articles found upon the traitor's person and retained in your care.

I have the honor to be,

Very respectfully,
SIMON CAMERON
Secretary of War.

Reply was made as follows.

HEADQUARTERS, CHEAT MOUNTAIN DIVISION,
HUTTONSVILLE, Oct. 30, 1861.

HON. SIMON CAMERON:

Sir:—Your letter of instruction of the 22d inst. is received. On further investigation it is made to appear that the three shots received by Colonel John A. Washington, all of which were plainly visible on his body, were fired by Sergeant John J. Weiler (not Leiber, as before reported), Corporal W. L. Birney, Private Wm. F. Johnson, all of Company E, Seventeenth Indiana Regiment. In accordance with the tenor of your letter of 22d inst. I have distributed the articles among these soldiers, Sergeant Weiler receiving the revolver.

Very respectfully,
Your obedient servant,
J. J. Reynolds,
Brigadier General

The remaining pistol being awarded to Sergeant Weiler, the large knife was given to Corporal Birney, the gauntlets to Private Johnson. General Reynolds took charge of the field glass, and subsequently gave it to Colonel Washington's son, George Washington, of Charles Town, West Virginia; Colonel Hascall took the spurs and Captain Levering the small powder flask. Reverend John T. Rose, son of Captain George S. Rose, assistant adjutant general, ended up with the letter that was mutilated by one of the bullets.[14]

On the afternoon of September 13, the Sixth North Carolina Infantry Regiment had approached the skirmishing area where the Tygart's Valley River crosses from the west to the east side of the valley and found that Union sharpshooters were making it rather lively for General Loring and his staff in a house where they had established headquarters.

First Lieutenant George Mills recalled that Company G, with a major in charge, was ordered to drive the Union riflemen out of range and that they marched across a field of high grass, reaching the river where its course closely hugged the foot of the mountain.

They made their way carefully under the natural cover until they had proceeded as far as they could without being discovered by the Federals and then climbed the mountain—pulling themselves up by bushes—until they reached the first ridge, where they could see all the way down the river to the Elkwater breastworks. The position loomed ominous, the works being covered with well-positioned batteries of artillery and literally bristling with muskets which strongly backed up heavy picket posts strung across the entire width of the valley.

The company was ordered to lie down and keep perfectly quiet as the Union sharpshooters were just below and within easy rifle range. Some of the men became impatient and threatened to open fire, but the major declared that he would kill the first man to make any noise. They lay there for half an hour watching the Yankee marksmen fire away at the Confederate officers up the valley. All at once the Federals started back to their works, a few of them stopping to knock apples from an apple tree.

Mills said his gallant commander raised up with a long drawn sigh and said, "Well boys, if we must, we must, so come on," and they marched down the hill again, coming out of a deep ravine only to find themselves face to face with a Union force ready to fire! The major promptly jumped off a ten-foot bank into the Tygart's Valley River calling on the company to follow, which order was promptly obeyed.

The line of trees follows Union entrenchments at Elkwater.

Retiring in good order they kept themselves well under the bank of the river for about a hundred yards, coming out on a sand bank, protected by a high fence.

The major ordered the company to hold position where they were while he went to headquarters to report their *success* and receive further orders. Taking one man with him, they started across the high grass field when a gun from one of the Union batteries fired a round, the shot passing high and harmlessly over the heads of all concerned. The major, believing his insignia of rank had drawn the fire, fell flat in the grass, quickly followed by his bodyguard; but scrambling up, soon made his way to headquarters, issued his report, and then asked to be relieved as he was very sick.

The company was ordered to remain at its post, with a strong picket posted at the ford and to hold it until morning. They spent the night miserably wet and cold but were favored with beautiful sunshine the next morning. In a short while, the picket at the ford became engaged with a squad of about twenty Federals working their way forward under the cover of the bank of the river; brisk fire was exchanged and two Confederates, John Dowdle and John F. Logan, were wounded, but the Union squad was forced to retire. The company then withdrew to a new position which was held until Loring retired and they were recalled.[15]

The Confederates above the Elkwater entrenchments, not enticed at the prospect of a frontal assault against the strong works, had started on the morning of September 13 to cut a road around the mountain in an attempt to outflank the Union position.

C. E. Taylor of Company F, Twenty-first Virginia Infantry Regiment, remembered that they sent twenty or thirty pioneers on the detail with an advance guard—of which he was a member—about a hundred yards in front of the work party as a security measure. The guard had orders to avoid rattling dry leaves, snapping a stick, or letting the sun shine on their guns. The road, about a mile long, was scheduled to be finished after dark on the fourteenth and the cannon dismounted, the carriages disassembled and carried to the end of the construction to be reassembled and ready for use on the morning of the fifteenth, but the work party and guard were recalled that night and rejoined the main body of troops.[16]

General Reynolds reported that the enemy was again in position on the fourteenth in front of Elkwater and a few rounds of artillery fire from a gun supported by a company of the Fifteenth Indiana Infantry was again administered and the Confederates retired as before.[17]

During the late afternoon and night of September 14, the Confederates withdrew from in front of Elkwater, making their way toward their Valley Mountain Camp in obedience to the following order issued by General Lee that morning:

HEADQUARTERS
Camp on Valley River, Va., September 14, 1861.

Special Orders
  No. ——

The forced reconnaissance of the enemy's positions, both at Cheat Mountain Pass [Summit] and Valley River, having been completed, and the character of the natural approaches and the nature of the artificial defenses exposed, the Army of the Northwest will resume its former position at such time and in such manner as General Loring shall direct, and continue its preparations for further operations. The commanding general experiences much gratification at the cheerfulness and alacrity displayed by the troops in this arduous operation. The promptitude with which they surmounted every difficulty, driving in and capturing the enemy's pickets on the fronts examined and exhibiting that readiness for attack, gives assurance of victory when a fit opportunity offers.

R. E. LEE,
General, Commanding[18]

Chapter Fourteen
Autumn Anguish

General Reynolds's report of September 17, 1861, found the Confederates retired from in front of the works on Cheat Summit as well as Elkwater and the campaign was ended.

Although the actual fighting of the campaign was of a small magnitude, a victory for Lee could have had most important results in northwestern Virginia. It could have changed the condition of state affairs so delicately balanced at that time and a Confederate victory could have had important bearing on subsequent military operations.

On September 17, General Lee wrote two letters, one to his wife and one to Governor John Letcher of Virginia. These letters are as near as he came to making a written report, although Jefferson Davis in a postwar address revealed that General Lee had made a verbal report to him, insisting that nothing be said publicly of it. Davis said that Lee stood in silence without defending himself or allowing others to defend him, for he was unwilling to offend anyone who was wearing a sword and striking blows for the Confederacy.[1]

> Valley Mount, September 17, 1861.
>
> I received, dear Mary, your letter of the 5th by Beverly Turner, who is a nice young soldier. I am pained to see fine young men like him, of education and standing, from all the old and respectable families in the State, serving in the ranks. I hope in time they will receive their reward. I met him as I was returning from an expedition to the enemy's works, which I had hoped to have surprised on the morning of the 12th, both at Cheat Mountain and on Valley River. All the attacking parties with great labour had reached their destination, over mountains considered impassable to bodies of troops, notwithstanding a heavy storm that set in the day before and raged all night, in which they had to stand up till daylight. Their arms were then unserviceable, and they in poor condition for a fierce assault against artillery and superior numbers. After waiting till 10 o'clock for the assault on Cheat Mountain, which did not take place, and which was to have been the signal for the rest, they were withdrawn, and, after waiting three days in front of the enemy, hoping he would come out of his trenches, we returned to our position at this place. I can not tell you my regret and mortification at the untoward

events that caused the failure of the plan. I had taken every precaution to ensure success and counted on it. But the Ruler of the Universe willed otherwise and sent a storm to disconcert a well-laid plan, and to destroy my hopes. We are no worse off now that before, except the disclosure of our plan, against which they will guard. We met with one heavy loss which grieves me deeply: Colonel Washington accompanied Fitzhugh on a reconnoitering expedition, and I fear they were carried away by their zeal and approached within the enemy's pickets. The first they knew was a volley from a concealed party within a few yards of them. Their balls passed through the Colonel's body, then struck Fitzhugh's horse, and the horse of one of the men was killed. Fitzhugh mounted the Colonel's horse and brought him off. I am much grieved. He was always anxious to go on these expeditions. This was the first day I assented. Since I had been thrown into such intimate relations with him, I had learned to appreciate him very highly. Morning and evening have I seen him on his knees praying to his Maker.

"The righteous perisheth and no man layeth it to heart, and the righteous is taken away from the evil to come."[2] May God have mercy on us all! I suppose you are at the Hot Springs, and will direct to you there. Our poor sick, I know, suffer much. They bring it on themselves by not doing what they are told. They are worse than children, for the latter can be forced. . . .

Truly yours,
R. E. LEE.[3]

Dr. Charles Quintard, chaplain of the First Tennessee Infantry Regiment, remembered that he saw General Lee just after he had learned of the death of Colonel Washington: "He was standing with his right arm thrown over the neck of his horse,—a blooded animal, thoroughly groomed—and I was impressed first of all by the man's splendid physique, and then by the look of extreme sadness that pervaded his countenance. He felt the death of his relative very keenly and seemed greatly dispirited.

"It was my high privilege later on to be brought in contact with this great and good man and to learn most thoroughly to appreciate his exalted character and to understand why his life is today an enduring inheritance of his country and of the Church of Christ. Personally he was a man of rare gifts, physical and mental. To these were added the advantages of finished culture. He was a very Bayard in manner and bearing.

The habits of temperance, frugality and self-control, formed
by him in youth, adhered to him through life."[4]

VALLEY MOUNTAIN, September 17, 1861.
My Dear Governor: I received your very kind note of the 5th
instant, just as I was about to accompany General Loring's command on an expedition to the enemy's works in front, or I would
have before thanked you for the interest you take in my welfare,
and your too flattering expressions of my ability. Indeed, you
overrate me much, and I feel humbled when I weigh myself by
your standard. I am, however, very grateful for your confidence,
and I can answer for my sincerity in the earnest endeavour I make
to advance the cause I have so much at heart, though conscious of
the slow progress I make. I was very sanguine of taking the
enemy's works on last Thursday morning. I had considered the
subject well. With great effort the troops intended for the surprise
had reached their destination, having traversed twenty miles of
steep, rugged mountain paths; and the last day through a terrible
storm, which lasted all night, and in which they had to stand
drenched to the skin in cold rain. Still their spirits were good.
When morning broke, I could see the enemy's tents on Valley
River, at the point on the Huttonsville road just below me. It was
a tempting sight. We waited for the attack on Cheat Mountain,
which was to be the signal. Till 10 A. M. the men were cleaning
their unserviceable arms. But the signal did not come. All chance
for a surprise was gone. The provision of the men had been de-
stroyed the preceding day by the storm. They had nothing to eat
that morning, could not hold out another day, and were obliged
to be withdrawn. The party sent to Cheat Mountain to take that
in rear had also to be withdrawn. The attack to come off from
the east side failed from the difficulties in the way; the opportunity was lost, and our plan discovered. It is a grievous dis-
appointment to me, I assure you. But for the rain-storm. I have
no doubt it would have succeeded. This Governor, is for your
own eye. Please do not speak of it; we must try again. Our greatest loss is the death of my dear friend, Colonel Washington. He
and my son were reconnoitering the front of the enemy. They
came unawares upon a concealed party, who fired upon them
within twenty yards, and the Colonel fell pierced by three balls.
My son's horse received three shots, but he escaped on the Colonel's horse. His zeal for the cause to which he had devoted himself carried him, I fear, too far. We took some seventy prisoners,
and killed some twenty-five or thirty of the enemy. Our loss was
small besides what I have mentioned. Our greatest difficulty is the
roads. It has been raining in these mountains about six weeks. It

Lieutenant Colonel Washington's monument.

Mountain from which Lee looked down on Union Elkwater camp.

is impossible to get along. It is that which has paralysed all our
efforts. With sincere thanks for your good wishes,

I am very truly yours,

R. E. LEE[5]

His Excellency, Governor John Letcher.

Many of the Confederate soldiers were displeased with the
results of the campaign after their arduous efforts. The Confederate doctor, J. R. Buist, with Anderson's Tennessee Brigade said: "Well, at the end of seven day's marching and
starvation, we go back to Valley Mountain, the whole affair
having proved a failure—in the opinion of our brigade, chiefly
from the old fogyism and want to pluck among the Virginians. Never were men more sick of Virginia and Virginians
than we are."[6]

As Donelson's brigade made its weary way back to camp,
word was out that General Loring had failed to perform his
part of the plan and that his excuse was that the rain and
high waters prevented him carrying out his assignment. As
the brigade moved down the road they passed the general's
advance field headquarters and Albert Tavel of the Eighth
Tennessee Infantry Regiment remembered: "He 'popped'
upon a stump and stood as erect as a cock partridge in August, and gave the passing soldiers a grand military review. He
wore a black suit of corduroy goods with a broad rimmed hat
set on the side of his head, topped off with a flaming feather
or cockade plume. Our men had been instructed to salute the
General as they passed, but if a single man in the ranks did
any such thing we did not see or hear of it. . . . Not a voice
was raised, not an old hat lifted as we sullenly passed by."[7]

In contrast, two days earlier on the same weary trip back,
this same brigade had made the mountains ring with cheer
after cheer for Robert E. Lee when he had ridden into their
midst.

The Kanawha Valley Campaign had continued during the
time that Lee had been occupied with the Cheat Mountain
movements and General William S. Rosecrans had moved
from Clarksburg by way of Weston, Sutton, and Summersville to reinforce General Cox, and on September 10, had
attacked General Floyd's entrenched position at Carnifex

Ferry. Floyd succeeded in beating back several charges by Rosecrans's command but darkness had ended the conflict. He considered the Union force in front of him overwhelming, plus the fact that Wise, whom he had summoned to his aid, had not shown up; so accordingly, during the night he fell back to the south bank of the Gauley River.

Floyd again ordered Wise to reinforce him and this time Wise obeyed, but before he could reach him he was ordered to return as Floyd, in a sudden change of mind, was retreating farther eastward.

On September 14, Floyd had retreated to the western summit of Big Sewell Mountain. Wise had proceeded him—under orders—and halted about a mile east of Floyd on the eastern summit of the same mountain.

On September 16, Floyd held a council of war and invited Wise, who, during the meeting, argued that he held the stronger position and urged Floyd to concentrate all the troops on the high ground he occupied. Floyd seemed to agree, the council ended and Wise returned to his own camp. He had no sooner arrived when Floyd's column began to pass through and soon a note from Floyd was received saying that he had decided to retreat to the vicinity of Meadow Bluff, some twelve miles to the rear, and Wise was ordered to cover the movement. Wise was outraged and refused to obey the order with repeated inquiries and orders from Floyd failing to budge him.[8]

With the Cheat Mountain Campaign ended, General Lee decided to join Wise and Floyd, hoping to restore harmony between the two, and to resist further advance of the enemy or drive him back if possible. He ordered Loring to leave a sufficient force to watch the enemy at Cheat Mountain and to follow with the rest of the army, joining him as soon as possible.

General Lee rode out of Valley Mountain with Captain Taylor and a small cavalry escort—disheartened and discredited by many. Southern cynics called him "Granny Lee" and took him to task for his failure and alleged lack of decision. Lee's stock was never lower in the Confederacy and his career was almost ruined before it really started.

E. A. Pollard, Southern historian and editor of the *Richmond Examiner,* wrote: "The most remarkable circumstances of this campaign was, that it was conducted by a general who had never fought a battle, who had a pious horror of guerrilas, and whose extreme tenderness of blood induced him to depend exclusively upon the resources of strategy, to essay the achievement of victories without the cost of life."[9]

On September 21, General Lee arrived in Floyd's Meadow Bluff camp. Thus, he found Wise about twelve miles in advance of Floyd with the Wise legion confronted by Rosecrans's entire army.

Lee rode forward on the twenty-second and saw that Wise's position was the most favorable place to make a stand, being naturally a strong point. He returned to Floyd's camp, weighed the reports of enemy activities and on the twenty-fourth started for Wise's position ordering four of Floyd's regiments brought to that place immediately. Rosecrans occupied a position about a mile from Wise on the same crest that Floyd had positioned himself earlier.

The next day, September 25, a messenger arrived with an order from President Davis relieving General Wise of his command and ordering him to return to Richmond immediately.

On the twenty-ninth Loring's army began arriving and was ordered to join Lee who was facing Rosecrans and expecting to be attacked at anytime; but on the morning of October 6, 1861, it was learned that Rosecrans had withdrawn during the night. Lee attempted pursuit, but because of the roads and condition of his troops, called off the operation and returned to camp.

General Lee remained until the last of October but due to the lateness of the season and the impassability of the roads decided that further operations would be useless. Thus, the campaign in West Virginia was virtually concluded and Lee started toward Richmond.

The Cheat Mountain Campaign had failed and Lee had not won a foot of northwest Virginia from the Federals. The Kanawha operation, as well, was considered a failure and at its conclusion a large portion of the state was in possession of the Union, including the Kanawha and Ohio River valleys.[10]

Fate had seemingly dealt Lee a severe blow, but in seven months, fate struck again. This time in the form of a Union bullet and shell fragment that put General Joseph E. Johnston out of the saddle as well as the Peninsular Campaign and spelled opportunity for Robert E. Lee. About twenty hours later, on June 1, 1862, he was given command of the Army of Northern Virginia—a charge he never relinquished until Appomattox—and launched one of the most illustrious careers of any military commander in all of history.

Appendixes

Appendix A
Notes

Chapter One
Misgiving in the Mountains
Pages 1-13

1. War Records Office, *War of the Rebellion, a Compilation of the Official Records of the Union and Confederate Armies 1880 to 1901,* Volume 2, p. 802. Hereafter cited as O.R.; unless otherwise stated, all references will be to Series I.

2. O.R., Volume 2, pp. 843, 855, 873.

3. O.R., Volume 2, pp. 51-52.

4. O.R., Volume 2, p. 237.

5. *Battles and Leaders of the Civil War,* Volume 1, pp. 138-39. Hereafter cited as B.&L.

6. O.R., Volume 2, p. 981.

7. O.R., Volume 2, p. 245.

8. O.R., Volume 2, p. 986. Note: Mailing's Bottom was probably meant to be Marlin's Bottom.

9. O.R., Volume 2, p. 987.

10. *Confederate Military History,* Volume 11, pp. 203-4. Hereafter cited as C.M.H.

11. C.M.H., Volume 3, p. 153.

12. Stephen Lee not to be confused with Stephen D. Lee.

13. O.R., Volume 5, p. 6.

14. C.M.H., Volume 3, p. 153.

Chapter Two
Sanctuary on Cheat
Pages 14-31

1. John Beatty, *Memoirs of a Volunteer,* p. 31. Hereafter cited as Beatty.

2. David Stevenson, *Indiana's Roll of Honor,* Volume 1, p. 154. Hereafter cited as Stevenson.

3. John Levering, *Lee's Advance and Retreat in the Cheat Mountain Campaign in 1861,* pp. 13-14. Hereafter cited as Levering.

4. J. T. Pool, *Under Canvas,* pp. 16-17. Hereafter cited as Pool.

5. William Landon, "The Fourteenth Indiana Regiment on Cheat Mountain; Letters to the Vincennes Sun," *Indiana Magazine of History* 29 (December 1933): 350-71. Hereafter cited as Landon, I.M.H. 29.

6. Pool, p. 12.

7. Landon, I.M.H. 29, p. 352.

Notes—Pages 21-49

8. Stevenson, p. 159-60.
9. Landon, I.M.H. 29, p. 353.
10. Charles H. Ross, "Scouting for Bushwhackers in West Virginia in 1861," pp. 399-400. Hereafter cited as Ross.
11. Beatty, pp. 31, 34-35.
12. Ross, pp. 399-401.
13. Landon, I.M.H. 29, p. 353.
14. Stevenson, p. 157.
15. Ebenezer Hannaford, *The Story of a Regiment*, p. 539. Hereafter cited as Hannaford.
16. Stevenson, pp. 156-58.
17. Augustus M. Van Dyke, "Early Days," pp. 24-25. Hereafter cited as Van Dyke.
18. Same.
19. Catherine Merrill, *The Soldier of Indiana in the War for the Union*, p. 78. Hereafter cited as Merrill.
20. Pool, pp. 18-19, 45.
21. Pool, pp. 34-35.

Chapter Three
Bushwhackers in the Laurel
Pages 32-60

1. Stevenson, p. 161.
2. William T. Price, "Guerrilla Warfare," *West Virginia Historical Magazine Quarterly* 4 (July 1904): 242-43. Note: Other sources disagree as to number and kind of casualties.
3. Landon, I.M.H. 29, p. 355.
4. Pool, pp. 22-23.
5. Charles Leib, *Nine Months in the Quartermaster Department*.
6. O.R., Volume 2, pp. 984-85.
7. O.R., Volume 51, Part 2, p. 1061; Volume 33, pp. 1081-83, 1252-53.
8. O.R., Volume 2, pp. 984-85.
9. Stevenson, p. 162.
10. Landon, I.M.H. 29, pp. 355-56; Pool, pp. 27-28; Charles H. Ross, "Old Memories," p. 152. Hereafter cited as Ross, Old Memories.
11. Pool, p. 29.
12. C.M.H., Volume 3, p. 154.
13. C.M.H., Volume 3, pp. 154-55.
14. C.M.H., Volume 3, p. 154.
15. O.R., Volume 51, Part 2, p. 206.
16. Merrill, pp. 105-34.
17. Stevenson, pp. 155-56.

Notes—Pages 49-65

18. Beatty, p. 51.
19. Beatty, p. 44.
20. Beatty, p. 45.
21. Stevenson, p. 163.
22. Merrill, pp. 79-80.
23. Landon, I.M.H. 29, p. 359.
24. Stevenson, pp. 163-64.
25. Beatty, pp. 48-49.
26. A. C. Jones, "The Mountain Campaign Failure," *Confederate Veteran* 22 (July 1914) and 22 (August 1914). Hereafter cited as Jones, C.V.M.
27. John Henry Cammack, *Personal Recollections*, p. 34. Hereafter cited as Cammack.
28. Beatty, pp. 52-54.
29. George H. Mills, "Supplemental Sketch, Sixteenth Regiment," in *Histories and Battalions from North Carolina in the Great War, 1861-65*, ed. Walter Clark, Volume 4, pp. 142-43. Hereafter cited as Mills.
30. Beatty, pp. 57, 61.

Chapter Four
Field of Forlorn Hope
Pages 61-71

1. O.R., Series IV, Volume 1, pp. 242-43.
2. O.R., Series IV, Volume 1, p. 294.
3. O.R., Series IV, Volume 1, pp. 231-32, 272.
4. O.R., Volume 2, p. 827.
5. Ezra J. Warner, *Generals in Gray*, p. 181.
6. O.R., Series IV, Volume 1, p. 255.
7. O.R., Series IV, Volume 1, pp. 342-43.
8. O.R., Volume 2, p. 504.
9. Robert E. Lee, Jr., *Recollections and Letters of General Robert E. Lee*, p. 55. Hereafter cited as R. E. Lee, Jr.
10. Davis was mistaken here as Loring was not at Valley Mountain at this time.
11. Jefferson Davis, *The Rise and Fall of the Confederate Government*, Volume 1, p. 434. Hereafter cited as Davis.
12. Walter H. Taylor, *Four Years with General Lee*, p. 16. Hereafter cited as Walter H. Taylor. R. E. Lee, Jr., p. 40.
13. R. E. Lee, Jr., pp. 40-41. (The White House Plantation was Lee's son, Fitzhugh's, place on the Pamunkey River.)
14. Walter H. Taylor, pp. 35-36.

Notes—Pages 65-84

15. Douglass Southall Freeman, *R. E. Lee: A Biography*, Volume 1, pp. 541-42. Hereafter cited as Freeman.

16. Isaac Hermann, *Memoirs of a Veteran Who Served as a Private in the 60's in the War Between the States*, p. 38.

17. C.M.H., Volume 6, pp. 426-27.

18. Charles Todd Quintard, *Doctor Quintard, Chaplain, C.S.A.*, p. 17. Hereafter cited as Quintard.

19. Mills, p. 140.

20. Brackets mine.

21. R. E. Lee, Jr., pp. 38-39.

22. Walter H. Taylor, p. 16.

Chapter Five
Commander or Coordinator
Pages 72-81

1. O.R., Volume 5, p. 767.

2. O.R., Volume 5, pp. 828-29.

3. O.R., Volume 5, p. 193.

4. O.R., Series IV, Volume 1, p. 631. The records also show Loring appointed to command July 20, 1861, O.R., Volume 51, Part 2, p. 180. Abstract of October 1861, Volume 5, p. 933, lists him as commanding Army of the Northwest.

5. Davis, p. 309.

6. A. L. Long, *Memoirs of Robert E. Lee, His Military and Personal History*, p. 120. Hereafter cited as Long.

7. Long, pp. 120-21.

8. B. H. Cathey, "Additional Sketch Sixteenth [North Carolina] Regiment," in *Histories and Battalions from North Carolina in the Great War, 1861-65*, ed. Walter Clark, Volume 4, p. 753.

9. R. E. Lee, Jr., pp. 39-41.

10. C.M.H., Volume 3, p. 155.

11. Walter H. Taylor, p. 16.

12. Freeman, p. 559.

Chapter Six
Costly Courtesy
Pages 82-90

1. Long, pp. 121-22.

2. Long, pp. 122-23.

3. Walter H. Taylor, p. 23.

*Notes—*Pages 84-108

4. Garnett Andrews, "A Battle Planned Not Fought," *Confederate Veteran Magazine* 5 (June 1897): 294.

5. Jones, C.V.M.

6. Freeman, pp. 552-53.

7. M. B. Toney, *Privations of a Private*, pp. 20-21.

8. John H. Worsham, *One of Jackson's Foot Cavalry*, pp. 15-16.

9. Eva Margaret Carnes, "George W. (Bishop) Peterkin at Valley Mountain," *Randolph County Historical Society Magazine of History and Biography* 12 (April 1961): 97-98. Hereafter cited as Carnes, R.C.H.S.M. 12.

10. Freeman, pp. 577-78.

Chapter Seven
Measles and Mud
Pages 91-100

1. Walter H. Taylor, p. 17. Brackets mine.

2. Mills, p. 142; Harrill, p. 771.

3. Brackets mine.

4. R. E. Lee, Jr., pp. 41-42.

5. Freeman, p. 557; Pool, p. 33.

6. Worsham, p. 17.

7. Carnes, R.C.H.S.M. 12, pp. 97-98.

8. Ruth Woods Dayton, *The Diary of a Confederate Soldier, James E. Hall*, p. 19. Hereafter cited as Dayton.

9. Walter H. Taylor, p. 17.

10. Mills, pp. 142-43.

11. Walter A. Clark, *Under the Stars and Bars; or, Memories of Four Years Service with the Oglethorpes, of Augusta, Georgia*, p. 22. Hereafter cited as Clark.

12. Worsham, p. 16.

13. Dayton, p. 20.

Chapter Eight
Kanawha Conflict
Pages 101-11

1. B.&L., Volume 1, p. 143.

2. O.R., Volume 5, p. 766.

3. O.R., Volume 5, pp. 773-77.

4. O.R., Volume 5, pp. 780-81.

5. B.&L. Volume 1, p. 143.

6. O.R., Volume 5, pp. 782-86.

Notes—Pages 108-25

7. O.R., Volume 5, p. 788.
8. O.R., Volume 5, pp. 790-91.
9. O.R., Volume 5, pp. 794-96.
10. B.&L., Volume 1, p. 143.
11. O.R., Volume 5, pp. 799-800.
12. O.R., Volume 5, p. 802.
13. O.R., Volume 5, pp. 804-5.
14. O.R., Volume 5, pp. 115, 806, 815-16.
15. B.&L., Volume 1, p. 143; O.R., Volume 5, p. 809.
16. O.R., Volume 5, p. 810.
17. O.R., Volume 5, pp. 836-37.
18. Walter H. Taylor, *General Lee, His Campaigns in Virginia 1861-1865*, pp. 33-34.
19. B.&L., Volume 1, pp. 144-45.

Chapter Nine
Gentle Persuasion
Pages 112-25

1. O.R., Volume 51, Part 2, pp. 283-84. Note that the First Georgia Infantry Regiment was brigaded in the Third Brigade which consisted of regiments based in the Valley Mountain area except for the First Georgia which was based on the Greenbrier River Camp at Bartow.
2. The location of General Reynolds's headquarters varies with different accounts, some saying the location was at Cheat Mountain Pass, others saying Elkwater. Actually his headquarters was located both places at various times.
3. Theodore F. Lang, *Loyal West Virginia from 1861 to 1865*, pp. 47-48. Hereafter cited as Lang.
4. Brackets mine. O.R., Volume 51, Part 2, pp. 282-83.
5. Walter H. Taylor, p. 20.
6. Parentheses mine.
7. Thomas A. Head, *Campaigns and Battles of the Sixteenth Regiment, Tennessee Volunteers*, p. 35. Hereafter cited as Head.
8. Lang, p. 48.
9. O.R., Volume 5, p. 192. Note: Walter Taylor says this order issued on Sept. 9, 1861.
10. O.R., Volume 5, pp. 188-89.
11. O.R., Volume 5, p. 189. Note: Wounded man was the only Union casualty, Private Frank Connor, Company G, Third Ohio Infantry.
12. Same.
13. Stevenson, pp. 169-71.
14. Stevenson, p. 169.

Chapter Ten
Rendezvous in the Rain
Pages 126-45

1. Cammack, p. 35; George E. Moore, ed., "A Confederate Record," *West Virginia History* 22 (July 1961): 206. Hereafter cited as G. Moore, W.Va.H. 22.

2. Note: Some accounts differ slightly as to the various starting times, but these seem to be the ones most generally accepted.

3. C.M.H., Volume 3, p. 159.

4. Walter H. Taylor, p. 23; O.R., Volume 51, Part 2, p. 285. Special Orders No. 113 lists Major Boykin as commanding Thirty-first Virginia Infantry Regiment on this date.

5. Cammack, p. 36; G. Moore, W.Va.H. 22, p. 206.

6. Head, p. 32; Dr. J. W. Gray, *The Nashville Union and American*, December 5, 1861. Hereafter cited as Gray.

7. Albert B. Tavel, *Cheat Mountain or, Unwritten Chapter of The Late War, By a Member of the Bar*, p. 63. Hereafter cited as Tavel.

8. Tavel, pp. 65-66.

9. Tavel, pp. 64-68.

10. J. J. Womack, *The Diary of Captain J. J. Womack*, pp. 15-16. Hereafter cited as Womack. Note: The farm owner's name was Winnan. There were people in this same area whose name was Wynan. It is not known if these two different spellings were actually two different families or spelling variations of one family.

11. Head, p. 34.

12. Head, p. 36; Gray.

13. Head, p. 36.

14. Gray; Womack, p. 16. (Womack says there were only three pickets: 1 killed, 1 mortally wounded, 1 escaped.)

15. Gray; Womack, p. 16 (Womack says four in number, all surrendered); Tavel, p. 70 (Tavel says two captured, two killed).

16. Head, p. 36; Gray.

17. Gray. Neither Head nor Womack mention this incident.

18. Gray. Head does not mention this incident. Womack says some out fishing and all escaped.

19. Head, p. 39. (Tavel, p. 91, says the guns were securely hid rather than distributed.)

20. Tavel, p. 72.

21. Dr. J. R. Buist, Letter to his uncle, *National Intelligencer*, November 23, 1861. Hereafter cited as Buist.

22. Note: "Gutta-Percha"—A tough plastic substance from the latex of several Malaysian trees resembling rubber but containing more resin. Used as insulation and in dentistry.

23. Buist.

Notes—Pages 143-65

   24. O.R., Volume 5, p. 188.
   25. Stevenson, p. 172.
   26. Clark, pp. 21-22.
   27. Levering, p. 22.
   28. Pool, p. 40; Levering, p. 22.
   29. Pool, p. 37.

Chapter Eleven
Misfires and Failures
Pages 146-70

   1. Walter H. Taylor, p. 27.
   2. C.M.H., Volume 3, p. 161.
   3. C.M.H., Volume 3, p. 161-62.
   4. Levering, p. 26.
   5. C.M.H., Volume 3, p. 162.
   6. Stevenson, p. 176. (Pool says the wagon master followed, p. 38.)
   7. O.R., Volume 5, pp. 186-87.
   8. Frank Moore, ed., *The Rebellion Record*, Volume 3, p. 137. Hereafter cited as Frank Moore.
   9. Pool, p. 37.
   10. O.R., Volume 5, p. 191.
   11. Jones, C.V.M. Note: Brackets mine.
   12. Cammack, p. 37.
   13. Tavel, pp. 77-78. Note: Buck and ball cartridges were of a paper-wrapped charge containing three buckshot and one full caliber ball.
   14. Head, p. 43.
   15. Levering, p. 25.
   16. Walter H. Taylor, pp. 28-29.
   17. Head, p. 46; R. E. Lee, Jr., pp. 46-47. (Note: Womack says earlier, p. 16.)
   18. Head, p. 47.
   19. Tavel, p. 79.
   20. Levering, p. 23.
   21. Pool, p. 40.
   22. Levering, p. 23.
   23. Pool, p. 40.
   24. Levering, p. 24; Pool, p. 40.
   25. Levering, p. 24.
   26. Pool, pp. 40-41.
   27. Levering, p. 24.
   28. O.R., Volume 5, p. 190.
   29. Dayton, pp. 36-37. Note: This was probably because of the 44th's part at the Battle of Rich Mountain.
   30. Lavender Ray, "The Letters of Lavender Ray," compiled and

Notes—Pages 165-84

edited by his daughter, Mrs. Ruby Felder Ray Thomas, Georgia Department of Archives and History. Hereafter cited as Ray.

31. Clark, pp. 24-25.

32. Brackets mine. Note: Lt. Merrill, a Union engineer officer was also captured about this time.

33. Same.

34. Quintard, p. 23.

35. Buist.

36. O.R., Volume 5, p. 187; Frank Moore, Volume 3, p. 138.

37. O.R., Volume 5, p. 187.

38. Levering, p. 25.

39. Levering, p. 14; Stevenson, p. 174. Note: Levering says Reynolds's headquarters were moved to Elkwater.

40. Stevenson, pp. 174-75, 177.

Chapter Twelve
Silent Defeat
Pages 171-78

1. Long, pp. 123-24.

2. Walter H. Taylor, p. 28.

3. Quintard, p. 24; Buist.

4. Ray, p. 12.

5. Stevenson, p. 174.

6. O.R., Volume 5, p. 187.

7. Pool, p. 24.

8. O.R., Volume 5, p. 185.

9. O.R., Volume 5, pp. 191-92. Brackets mine.

10. Walter H. Taylor, p. 29.

Chapter Thirteen
Standoff in the Valley
Pages 179-95

1. Stevenson, p. 178.

2. Joseph W. Keifer, *Slavery and Four Years of War*, p. 222. Hereafter cited as Keifer.

3. Stevenson, pp. 178-79.

4. Keifer, p. 222; Stevenson, p. 179.

5. O.R., Volume 5, pp. 185-86.

6. Brackets mine.

7. Same.

8. Same.

9. Same.

Notes—Pages 185-203

10. Ray. Brackets mine. Note: The guard was probably composed of five men from each company as two regiments had a total of twenty companies.

11. Clark, p. 27.

12. Pool, p. 44.

13. Tavel, pp. 81-83.

14. Levering, pp. 29-34.

15. Mills, pp. 144-46.

16. Charles E. Taylor, "War Letters To His Brother," *Wake Forest Student*, 1916.

17. O.R., Volume 5, p. 186.

18. O.R., Volume 5, pp. 192-93.

Chapter Fourteen
Autumn Anguish
Pages 196-204

1. R. E. Lee, Jr., pp. 52-53.

2. Isaiah 57:1. Lee was quoting from the Bible.

3. R. E. Lee, Jr., pp. 44-46.

4. Quintard, p. 30.

5. R. E. Lee, Jr., pp. 46-47.

6. Buist.

7. Tavel, pp. 86-87.

8. Freeman, pp. 585-86.

9. Edward A. Pollard, *The First Year of the War*, p. 168.

10. Walter H. Taylor, p. 35.

Appendix B
Bibliography

Andrew, Garnett. "A Battle Planned but Not Fought." *Confederate Veteran* 5 (June 1897).

Beatty, John. *Memoirs of a Volunteer.* New York: W. W. Norton & Company, Inc., 1946. 317 pp.

Buist, Dr. J. R. "Letter to his uncle." *National Intelligencer,* November 22, 1861, p. 2, col. 3.

Cammack, John Henry. *Personal Recollections.* Huntington, W. Va.: Paragon Printing and Publishing Co., 1923. 164 pp.

Carnes, Eva Margaret. "George W. (Bishop) Peterkin at Valley Mountain." *Randolph County Historical Society Magazine of History and Biography* 12 (April 1961).

Cathey, B. H. "Additional Sketch, Sixteenth Regiment." In *Histories of the Several Regiments and Battalions from North Carolina in the Great War, 1861-65,* edited by Walter Clark. vol. 4. Goldsboro: Nash Brothers, 1901.

Clark, Walter A. *Under the Stars and Bars; or, Memories of Four Years Service with the Oglethorpes, of Augusta, Georgia.* Augusta: Chronicle Printing Co., 1900. 239 pp.

Davis, Jefferson. *The Rise and Fall of the Confederate Government.* 2 vols. New York, 1881.

Dayton, Ruth Woods, ed. *The Diary of a Confederate Soldier, James E. Hall.* Charleston: Education Foundation, 1961. 141 pp.

Evans, Clement A., ed. *Confederate Military History.* 12 vols. Atlanta: Confederate Publishing Co., 1899.

Freeman, Douglass Southall. *R. E. Lee: A Biography.* vol. 1. New York: Charles Scribner's, ca. 1934, 1936.

Gray, Dr. J. W. *The Nashville Union and American,* December 5, 1861, Nashville, Tenn.

Hannaford, Ebenezer. *The Story of a Regiment: A History of the Campaigns, and Associations in the Field, of the Sixth Regiment Ohio Volunteer Infantry.* Cincinnati: The Author, 1868. 622 pp.

Head, Thomas A. *Campaigns and Battles of the Sixteenth Regiment, Tennessee Volunteers, ... 1861-1865.* Nashville: Cumberland Presbyterian Publishing House, 1885. 488 pp. illus.

Hermann, Isaac. *Memoirs of a Veteran Who Served as a Private in the 60's in the War Between the States. Personal Incidents, Experiences and Observations.* Atlanta, Ga.: Byrd Printing Co., 1911. 285 pp.

Johnson, R. U., and Buel, C. C., eds. *Battles and Leaders of the Civil War*. 4 vols. Atlanta: Confederate Publishing Co., 1884-1887.

Jones, A. C. "The Mountain Campaign Failure." *Confederate Veteran* 22 (July 1914), 22 (August 1914).

Keifer, Joseph Warren. *Slavery and Four Years of War. A Political History of Slavery in the United States, Together with a Narrative of the Campaigns and Battles of the Civil War*. 2 vols. New York: G. P. Putnam's Sons, The Knickerbocker Press, 1900.

Landon, William. "The Fourteenth Indiana Regiment on Cheat Mountain: Letters to the Vincennes Sun." *Indiana Magazine of History* 29 (December 1933).

Lang, Theodore F. *Loyal West Virginia from 1861 to 1865*. Baltimore: Deutsch Publishing Co., 1895. 382 pp.

Lee, Robert E. (Captain). *Recollections and Letters of General Robert E. Lee, By his Son*. New York, 1904.

Leib, Charles. *Nine Months in the Quarter-Master's Department: Or, The Chances for Making a Million*. Cincinnati: Moore, Wilstach, Keys & Co., 1862. 200 pp.

Levering, John. *Lee's Advance and Retreat in the Cheat Mountain Campaign in 1861: Supplemented by the Tragic Death of Colonel John A. Washington of His Staff*. In Military Order of the Loyal Legion of the United States. Illinois Commandery. *Military Essays and Recollections*. vol. 4. Chicago: Cozzens & Bealton Co., 1907.

Long, A. L. *Memoirs of Robert E. Lee, His Military and Personal History*. New York: J. M. Stoddard; Richmond: B. F. Johnson, 1886. 707 pp.

Merrill, Catherine. *The Soldier of Indiana in the War for the Union*. Indianapolis: Merrill and Co., 1864. 142 pp.

Mills, George H. "Supplemental Sketch, Sixteenth Regiment." In *Histories of the Several Regiments and Battalions from North Carolina in the Great War, 1861-65*, edited by Walter Clark. vol. 4. Goldsboro: Nash Brothers, 1901.

Moore, Frank, ed. *The Rebellion Record: A Diary of American Events, with Documents, Narratives, Illustrative Incidents, Poetry, Etc*. New York: G. P. Putnam, 1861.

Moore, George E., ed. "A Confederate Journal." *West Virginia History* 22 (July 1961).

Pollard, Edward A. *Southern History of the War*. 2 vols. New York: Charles B. Richardson, 1866.

Pool, J. T. *Under Canvas, Or, Recollections of the Fall and Summer Campaign of the 14th Regiment Indiana Volunteers, Col. Nathan Kimball, Western Virginia, in 1861*. Terre Haute: Oliver Barlett, Publisher, 1862. 64 pp.

Price, W. T. "Guerrilla Warfare, The Ambush on Greenbrier River in Which Seven Troopers Were Killed." *West Virginia Historical Magazine Quarterly* 4 (July 1904).

Quintard, Charles Todd. *Doctor Quintard, Chaplain, C. S. A. and Second Bishop of Tennessee; Being His Story of the War (1861-1865).* Edited and Extended by the Rev. Arthur Howard Noll. Sewanee, Tenn.: The University Press, 1905. 183 pp.

Ray, Lavender. "The Letters of Lavender Ray." Georgia Department of Archives and History. Compiled and edited by his daughter, Mrs. Ruby Felder Ray Thomas. Atlanta, Georgia.

Ross, Charles H. "Old Memories." In Military Order of the Loyal Legion of the United States, Wisconsin Commandery. *War Papers.* vol. 1. Milwaukee: Burdick, Armitage & Allen, 1891.

Ross, Charles H. "Scouting for Bushwhackers in West Virginia in 1861." In Military Order of the Loyal Legion of the United States, Wisconsin Commandery. *War Papers.* vol. 3. Milwaukee: Burdick & Allen, 1903.

Stevenson, David. *Indiana's Roll of Honor.* vol. 1. Indianapolis: The Author, 1864.

Tavel, Albert B. *Cheat Mountain Or, Unwritten Chapter of the Late War. By a Member of the Bar, Fayettesville, Tenn.* Nashville, 1885. 128 pp.

Taylor, Charles E. "War Letters to His Brother." *Wake Forest Student* March 1916.

Taylor, Walter H. *Four Years with General Lee.* New York: D. Appleton, 1878. 199 pp.

Taylor, Walter H. *General Lee, His Campaigns in Virginia 1861-1865.* Norfolk, 1906.

Toney, M. B. *Privations of a Private.* Nashville, 1905.

Van Dyke, Augustus M. "Early Days; Or the School of the Soldier." In Military Order of the Loyal Legion of the United States, Ohio Commandery. *Sketches of War History, 1861-1865.* vol. 5.

Warner, Ezra J. *Generals in Gray.* Louisiana State University Press, 1959. 420 pp.

War Records Office. *War of the Rebellion, A Compilation of the Official Records of the Union and Confederate Armies.* Compiled 1880-1901. Seventy volumes (in series) in 128 total volumes.

Womack, J. J. *The Diary of Captain J. J. Womack.* McMinnville, Tenn.: Womack Printing Co., 1961.

Worsham, John H. *One of Jackson's Foot Cavalry.* Jackson, Tenn.: McCowat-Mercer Press, Inc., 1964. 215 pp.

Appendix C
Consulted Works

Works consulted and though not cited may have influenced the writing.

"Active Service; or Campaigning in Western Virginia." *Continental Monthly* 1 (March 1861). New York.

Amann, William Frayne, ed. *Personnel of the Civil War.* 2 vols. New York: Thomas Yoseloff, ca. 1961.

Ambler, Charles H. "General R. E. Lee's Northwest Virginia Campaign." *West Virginia History* 5 (January 1944).

Barnwell, Robert W., Sr. "The First West Virginia Campaigns." *Confederate Veteran* 38 (April, May 1930).

Bierce, Ambrose. *Ambrose Bierce's Civil War.* Edited and with an Introduction by William McCann. Chicago: Henry Regnery Co., 1956.

Billings, John D. Hardtack and Coffee. *The Unwritten Story of Civil War Army Life.* Boston, 1887.

Chamberlayne, John Hampden. *Ham Chamberlayne-Virginian.* Richmond: Dietz Printing Co., 1932.

"Civil War Letters of Amory K. Allen." *Indiana Magazine of History* 31 (December 1935).

Culp, Edward C. *The 25th Ohio Vet. Vol. Infantry in the War for the Union.* Topeka, Kans.: G. W. Crane and Co., 1885.

Dowdey, Clifford, ed. *The Wartime papers of R. E. Lee.* Virginia Civil War Commission. Boston: Little, Brown and Company, ca. 1961.

Education Foundation, Inc. Charleston. *West Virginia in the Civil War.* (Charleston, 1958-   .)

Fry, Rose W. *Recollections of the Rev. John McElhenney, D.D.* Richmond: Whittet and Shepperson, 1893.

"General R. E. Lee at Cheat Mountain." *Confederate Veteran* 7 (March 1899).

Hagy, P. S. "The Cheat Mountain Campaign." *Confederate Veteran* 23 (March 1915).

McComb, William. "Tennesseeans in the Mountain Campaign, 1861." *Confederate Veteran* 22 (May 1914).

Maxwell, C. W. "Tommy Woods—Scout. A Story of Randolph in the Days of the Civil War." *West Virginia Review* 5 (August 1928).

Monfort, Elias R. *From Grafton to McDowell Through Tygart's Valley.* Cincinnati: H. C. Sherick, 1886.

Moore, George E. *A Banner in the Hills*. New York: Appleton-Century-Crofts, 1963.

Morgan, H. Wayne, ed. "A Civil War Diary of William McKinley." *The Ohio Historical Quarterly* 69 (July 1960).

Parker, Parson. "Sufferings of the Twelfth Georgia Regiment in the Mountains of Virginia." (n.p., 1862?.)

Poe, David. *Personal Reminiscences of the Civil War*. Buckhannon: Upshur Republican Print, 1911.

Price, Andrew. "Plain Tales of Mountain Trails." *West Virginia Blue Book*, 1928.

Purifay, John. "Letters on the West Virginia Campaigns." *Confederate Veteran* 34 (June 1926).

Stutler, Boyd B. "Death of Col. John Augustine Washington, C. S. A." *Randolph County Historical Society Magazine of History and Biography* 11 (1954).

Stutler, Boyd B. "Lee Fails in Mountain Campaign." *Randolph County Historical Society Magazine of History and Biography* 12 (April 1961).

White, Henry Alexander. *Robert E. Lee and the Southern Confederacy, 1807-1870*. New York: Putnam's, 1902.

Whittlesey, Charles. *War Memoranda, Cheat River to the Tennessee, 1861-1862*. Putnam's, 1902.

Index

223